DEFENSE STRATEGIES FOR THE SEVENTIES

WRITTEN UNDER THE AUSPICES OF
THE CENTER FOR INTERNATIONAL AFFAIRS
HARVARD UNIVERSITY

DEFENSE STRATEGIES FOR THE SEVENTIES

MORTON H. HALPERIN

LITTLE, BROWN AND COMPANY *Boston*

LIBRARY OF CONGRESS CATALOG CARD NO. 70-152452

FIRST PRINTING

Published simultaneously in Canada
by Little, Brown & Company (Canada) Limited

PRINTED IN THE UNITED STATES OF AMERICA

To David, Mark, and Gary

PREFACE

Does force, its employment and the threat of its employment, affect the behavior of nations and individuals? Despite the development of nuclear weapons, the answer seems clearly to be yes.

This book is based on the assumption that force continues to be used in international politics despite the development of thermonuclear weapons and intercontinental ballistic missiles.

Several absolute views about war in the current period contrast with the approach taken here. Holders of the first of these views argue that nuclear weapons have abolished war, that war has become impossible. Their line of thinking is that because nuclear weapons exist, all war would be total war; because no one wants total war, war will not take place. The events of the postwar period, however, clearly show that the invention of atomic weapons has not made war impossible. In fact, although major world war has been avoided, the amount of violence in the world has not been appreciably reduced. Nuclear weapons, then, have not abolished war; war very much remains an instrument of policy.

A second view suggests that although nuclear weapons have not yet made war impossible, war must be abolished if mankind is to survive. Those who hold this theory argue that unless war is abolished, we will eventually have a nuclear war that will destroy most, if not all, of civilization. This approach does not suggest how one can abolish war. Nor does it demonstrate that nuclear war is inevitable unless all violence is eliminated.

Supporters of a third, somewhat less extreme, approach contend that although war may continue, *nuclear* war has become "unthinkable." Nuclear war must be prevented if mankind is to survive. Some who have this opinion would argue that nuclear war should not be studied, for to study it is to allow that such a war is possible and acceptable and therefore likely. A contrary view — maintained throughout this book — holds that we are most likely to be able to prevent nuclear war if we study the subject carefully. In any case, the threat of nuclear war and of the use of nuclear weapons is significant in international politics. Even if, as appears likely, nuclear war never comes, the invention of nuclear weapons will have had a profound effect on international politics and, indeed, on human history.

A fourth, more extreme, approach advocates preventive nuclear war to produce peace, suggesting that a nuclear war is inevitable, and the sooner the better. Implicit in this theory is the belief that human violence can be ended but that preventive war, not international disarmament, is the means to this end.

All four approaches prescribe how nations should act, and all propose substantial changes. However, in this book changes in the behavior of nations in the nuclear age are described and changes that might improve security are suggested.

I have summarized the most important positions on each of the issues discussed, but inevitably my own view of the main choices open to American policy-makers has shaped the book's structure. I have defined military issues rather broadly, but I do not deal with many political questions that affect the role of military forces. The interaction between American forces in Europe and West Germany's policy toward Eastern Europe and the Soviet Union is not discussed, nor are American-Japanese relations. To do so would have greatly expanded this volume and taken us away from its primary subject. Vietnam is also not discussed in any systematic way. It has long since been clear that no strategic analysis can significantly clarify the Vietnam problem; moreover, any serious discussion of Vietnam would require a volume considerably larger than this one and would be obsolete in some measure before it was published.

Some of the material in this book appeared in my *Contemporary Military Strategy* (1967). Since completing that volume, I have worked for the federal government in the Defense Department and later on the staff of the National Security Council. The differences between *Defense Strategies for the Seventies* and the earlier book are in part due to changes in the world situation, but I suspect that they reflect much more what I have learned from my own experiences and what many learned from America's experiences in the second half of the 1960's.

Many individuals contributed in one way or another to this volume; they will know who they are. I will not burden the reader with a list, but I would be remiss if I did not again acknowledge the indispensable assistance of my wife.

Faithful readers (if there be any) of these prefaces may wish to know that Gary Isaac Halperin arrived on March 30, 1967. This book is dedicated to him and his two brothers with the hope that as they come to understand what their father does they will judge him kindly.

Morton H. Halperin

CONTENTS

CHAPTER ONE

THE ROLE OF FORCE IN THE NUCLEAR AGE 1

The Military Balance. The Effect of Military Power.

CHAPTER TWO

WARFARE IN THE NUCLEAR AGE 10

General War. Local War. Major Military Problems. General Nuclear War. The Defense of Local Areas.

CHAPTER THREE

QUANTITATIVE AND QUALITATIVE RESEARCH METHODS 28

Quantitative Methods. Qualitative Methods. The Interaction of Quantitative and Qualitative Analyses.

CHAPTER FOUR

THE EVOLUTION OF AMERICAN MILITARY STRATEGY 38

The Early Postwar Period. NSC 68 (1950). The Korean War. The New Look. Criticism of Massive Retaliation. Sputnik *and the Gaither Committee. 1960 Election. The McNamara Pentagon. The Nixon Doctrine and Sufficiency.*

CHAPTER FIVE

SOVIET MILITARY STRATEGY 54

Soviet General-War Strategy. Soviet Strategy for Europe. China.

CHAPTER SIX

CHINESE MILITARY STRATEGY 63

The Role of Force. Nuclear War. Conventional War.

CHAPTER SEVEN

GENERAL WAR: THE STRATEGY OF SUFFICIENCY 72

Assured Destruction. Crisis Stability. Relative Advantage. Damage Denial. Additional Sufficiency Issues. Specific Weapon Decisions. The Future of Land-based Missiles.

CHAPTER EIGHT

LIMITED WAR: THE NATURE OF THE LIMITING PROCESS 87

Determinants of Policy. The Limiting Process.

CHAPTER NINE

DETERRENCE AND DEFENSE IN EUROPE 99

The Soviet Military Threat. Alternative NATO Strategies.

CHAPTER TEN

DETERRENCE AND DEFENSE IN ASIA 113

Nuclear Weapons for Deterrence and Defense. Korea. Southeast Asia after Vietnam.

CHAPTER ELEVEN

ARMS CONTROL: SALT AND NPT 128

Strategic Arms Limitation Talks (SALT). Types of Agreement. Nonproliferation of Nuclear Weapons.

SELECTED BIBLIOGRAPHY 141

INDEX 147

DEFENSE STRATEGIES FOR THE SEVENTIES

CHAPTER ONE

THE ROLE OF FORCE IN THE NUCLEAR AGE

Through the ages, the evolution of technology for warfare has been marked by a search for, as well as a fear of, the absolute weapon, which, depending upon one's point of view, either would enable one state to dominate the world or would force all men to live in peace. Men have thought the crossbow, the machine gun, and the airplane to be such a weapon. The destruction of Hiroshima and Nagasaki led some people to describe the atomic bomb as the absolute weapon, but clearly the atomic bomb was not the ultimate weapon, and the search for it has proceeded to intercontinental missiles and submarine-launched missiles.

We are never likely to devise anything that can accurately be called an absolute weapon, but it is important to understand some of the changes in weapon technology that have followed the development of the atomic and then the hydrogen bomb — namely, changes in the destructive power of weapons and in the ability to deliver them. Unless one understands, at least generally, what changes technology has brought about, one cannot understand how the political problems of using or controlling force have changed.

The destructive power of a weapon should be thought of as a

yield to weight ratio — that is, the amount of destruction caused for each pound of explosive material. The base taken for comparing the destructive power of nuclear weapons is the weight of a TNT bomb that would cause the same amount of destruction as the nuclear weapon. The yield of an atomic bomb is expressed in the equivalent of one thousand pounds of TNT (kilotons) or one million pounds of TNT (megatons); that is, a two-megaton bomb has the equivalent destructive power of two million tons of TNT.

Twice during the nuclear age the destructive power of weapons increased enormously. The first atomic weapons, the so-called fission bombs, had a destructive power a thousand times greater per pound than traditional TNT and other high explosive weapons. The hydrogen or fusion bomb was a thousand times more powerful per pound than fission weapons. Thus, these two revolutions in fire power have produced a millionfold increase in power for a given weight.

Another way to indicate this changed magnitude of destruction is to say that one American bomber now carries more destructive power than that of all weapons used in all wars in human history. The largest bombs of World War II were the equivalent of approximately *five* tons of TNT, and the Hiroshima bomb was equal to approximately twenty thousand tons of TNT. Currently American nuclear weapons have yields from tenths of a kiloton to one million tons on the warhead of the *Minuteman* intercontinental missile and several million tons in large intercontinental bombers. Soviet warheads appear to have a similar range; the largest Soviet missile has a five-megaton warhead.

The fantastic increase in the destructive power of weapons has almost been matched by improvements in the ability to deliver these weapons. ICBMs possessed by the Soviet Union and by the United States can reach any point on the globe from any other point within thirty to forty minutes with incredible accuracy. This accuracy is expressed in terms of Circular Error Probability (CEP). The number identified as the CEP is the radius of a circle within which half of the fired weapons land. For example, if four missiles with a CEP of two miles were fired at a target, two of the missiles would land within two miles of the target. American and Soviet missiles appear to have a CEP of considerably less than two miles. Superpowers thus can fire missiles five thousand miles or more and have half of their missiles land within two miles of their target. The effectiveness of ICBMs will be further enhanced by the deployment of Multiple Independently Targeted Re-entry Vehicles. These warheads, known as MIRVs, enable each missile to carry several warheads, each of which can be accurately directed at a different target. The United States began deploying MIRVs in 1970, and the Soviets are believed to be working on MIRVs.

The Soviet Union has deployed a small Anti-Ballistic Missile (ABM) system around Moscow to shoot down incoming missiles, and the United States began deploying a small ABM system in 1969. These systems could somewhat reduce the number of missiles that can reach their target, but they would not alter the basic facts: both of the superpowers have thermonuclear weapons a million times more powerful than World War II weapons, and both can deliver these weapons with intercontinental missiles in about thirty minutes. These two general quantitative developments are important for understanding the impact of thermonuclear weapons on international politics.

In the period immediately after World War II these changes in technology were accompanied by a bipolar distribution of power between the United States and the Soviet Union. By the end of the 1960's, bipolarity had somewhat broken down; the substantial nuclear capability of the two superpowers was proving less relevant to the course of events than factors such as the conflict between the Soviet Union and China, the growing economic and political power of West Germany and Japan, and persistent nationalism in developing countries.

The Military Balance

Although analysts have argued about whether military force still has a role to play, governments have feared the results of inadequate military capability. Both the United States and the Soviet Union have spent large sums of money, perhaps exceeding the combined total of $100 billion, to develop nuclear forces and their delivery systems. To assess the role of nuclear weapons, it is important to have some understanding of the nuclear and conventional forces on both sides.

Strategic Nuclear Forces. Through the 1960's the American strategic nuclear force consisted of a large missile force and a moderate number of intercontinental bombers in addition to shorter range, fighter-bomber aircraft and missiles in Europe and perhaps elsewhere. The number of missiles in the American strategic nuclear arsenal has remained constant since the early 1960's and is likely to remain unchanged until at least the late 1970's. The United States has 1,000 *Minuteman* ICBMs and 54 *Titan* ICBMs. The *Minuteman* is a small solid-fueled missile kept in well-protected underground silos. Originally the *Minuteman* had one one-megaton warhead, but in 1970 the United States began to equip many of its *Minutemen* with a small number of MIRVs. The *Titan* is an older, larger liquid-fueled missile; it cannot be fired as quickly nor can it be as well protected as the *Minuteman*. The United States also has 41 submarines, each equipped with 16 missiles. In the late 1960's the original one-megaton warheads on some of the 656 *Polaris* missiles were replaced with three Multiple Re-entry Vehicles (MRV), which unlike MIRVs cannot be separately targeted. In 1970 the United States began to install *Poseidon* MIRV missiles in most of its missile-firing submarines. The United States also maintains a fleet of B-52 bombers, which has been gradually declining in numbers since the mid-1960's. In addition to these offensive forces American strategic capability includes an air defense system, and in 1970 the United States began to deploy a limited ABM system.

Soviet nuclear forces grew steadily during the 1960's. As of September 1969 the Soviet Union had surpassed the United States in number of land-based ballistic missiles and was producing *Polaris*-type submarines with 16 missiles each. The Soviets also had about 150 intercontinental bombers and an extensive air defense system as well as the small ABM system centered on Moscow.

Tactical Nuclear Forces. Since the mid-1950's the United States has built up an impressive array of so-called tactical nuclear weapons — that is, nuclear weapons designed to support land forces — in Europe and Asia. The United States has a capability in the form of nuclear weapons from extremely low yields — below that of the largest conventional weapons — to a kiloton and larger weapons for attacking air bases and other large targets. American stockpiles of tactical nuclear weapons in Europe grew steadily during the 1960's to a force of over seven thousand; these weapons are carried by a variety of delivery systems. The Soviets are reported to have a much smaller and less varied arsenal of tactical nuclear weapons consisting mainly of short-range rockets with warheads in the kiloton range. The Soviets also have over seven hundred medium-range missiles targeted against Western Europe.

Conventional Forces. Despite the growth of nuclear power and the increasing sophistication of the arsenals of the two superpowers, the United States and the Soviet Union as well as their allies have maintained large conventional ground forces. These forces might be employed along with tactical nuclear weapons, but they are also able to fight alone. All the major powers spend more than half of their military budget on conventional forces, much of it on salaries. Thus, along with their nuclear capabilities, the superpowers have a very real ability to fight conventionally.

The Effect of Military Power

We can consider the effect of military power on peacetime diplomacy, crises, conventional war, and nuclear war.

Peacetime Diplomacy. The great expense involved in developing large, sophisticated thermonuclear capabilities has been one of the prime reasons for the continuing of bipolarity. Only the United States and the Soviet Union have been able to afford many of these weapons. The United States, for example, spends on defense approximately three times the total United Kingdom budget and six times the British defense budget. Similar, perhaps greater, disparities exist between the Chinese and the American and Soviet budgets. Thus, although France, Great Britain, and China have begun to develop nuclear capabilities, the Soviet Union and the United States are — and are likely to remain for quite a while — the two superpowers.

Thermonuclear weapons have forced the two superpowers to take a new view of their relations. In a classic balance of power situation the two main powers would be in total conflict with each other and would seek support from other countries in an effort to tip the balance. However, particularly in the last several years, the two superpowers have come to see that although many things separate them, they are joined by a common desire to avoid thermonuclear war. This insight has led to pressure for détente in both the United States and the Soviet Union. The search for disarmament and arms-control agreements has changed in focus and emphasis from the attempt of idealists to create a world of total peace to an attempt by realists to improve the nature of the military balance and to reduce the likelihood of general nuclear war. Thus, in a world situation in which disagreement between the superpowers remains great, a partial test ban treaty and other measures, including the "hot line" agreement linking the United States and the Soviet Union with a high-speed, reliable communication system have been agreed to. The Strategic Arms Limitation Talks (SALT), which began in 1969, are the most dramatic and important manifestation of this trend. The greater emphasis on agreement between the two superpowers, particularly in arms control, must be attributed almost entirely to their destructive potentialities. Former Soviet Premier Nikita Khrushchev said, "The atom bomb recognizes no class differences."

Fear of thermonuclear war has led the superpowers to try to avoid situations of intense international political crisis. Both sides have refrained from pressing political advantages that might upset the military balance and have been extremely cautious in the use of conventional military forces. Thus, the Soviet Union has never employed its conventional capabilities to seize Berlin, and the United States has been restrained in its use of military force against Cuba. Various restraints on both sides have been operative, but fear of setting in motion a chain of events that might lead to general nuclear war has been dominant.

The same pressures have compelled the superpowers to become directly involved in local conflicts throughout the world. The Soviet Union and the United States believe that any conflict might precipitate general nuclear war. There has been a tendency, particularly on the part of the United States, to intervene quickly at the first sign of local conflict in order to isolate the conflict and to halt the fighting before it spreads to general war.

Crises. Caution has marked the approach of the superpowers to crises as well as to peacetime diplomacy. Both sides have sought to contain quickly any spontaneous crisis, such as the Hungarian uprising of 1956 and the Arab-Israeli wars. Even in crises induced by one of the superpowers — for example, the Cuban missile crisis in 1962 — both sides have acted in a cautious way designed to reduce the likelihood of general war and to end the conflict as quickly as possible. It is not that the superpowers and their allies have not sought to get political advantage from a crisis, but rather that their willingness to maneuver and to seek advantage has been severely limited by the overall military balance. In fact, the history of postwar crises suggests that the probability of nuclear war has been exaggerated and has tended to dominate the thinking of decision-makers during a crisis. One has only to recall Krushchev's statements during the Cuban missile crisis about the world being close to thermonuclear war or to read memoirs of American leaders at that time to realize the extent to which top leaders will allow this problem to influence their views. Because of the fear of a general nuclear war and the desire to end the conflict quickly, local conventional military power, which can be brought to bear quickly, has tended to be critical in crises such as those in Hungary and in Cuba.

Conventional War. Thermonuclear weapons have made extremely unlikely another large-scale military conflict of the order of World War I or World War II. Although neither of the superpowers has ruled out such a conflict in developing its military capabilities, neither seems to attach high priority to the probability of such a war. Nor if such a war were to occur, would it be likely to remain conventional and limited. Further, with the improbability of worldwide general war has come an increase in local conventional wars — both international and, more frequently, civil — for example, in Vietnam, Laos, Greece, and Korea. Such wars have all been fought under the shadow of the nuclear deterrent capability of the two superpowers; that is, the actions of the superpowers in these conflicts have been influenced by their belief that local conflicts could explode into general nuclear war. Though this phenomenon has led to the exercise of restraint on the part of the superpowers in the exploitation of success in local conflict, local conventional military forces and local political factors have nevertheless tended to dominate and determine the outcome of any particular military clash. Limited local wars, including guerrilla wars, have been an instrument of international political change and have become to a large extent the ultimate arbitrator of political conflict because nobody wants to use the real "ultimate" weapons — the nuclear weapons.

Nuclear War. The United States and the Soviet Union have been willing to allow conventional and local political factors to determine the outcome of much conflict in the postwar period precisely because this conflict does not threaten their vital interests. However, it is clear that nuclear weapons would remain the final arbiter when and if their vital interests were challenged. The major powers compete with each other in nonmilitary ways and in the use of conventional military force but with no hope of total military victory. We must try to live in peaceful coexistence with potential adversaries because we live in a world in which war cannot be abolished because there is no other means to settle issues that men feel are worth fighting for. But war — at least general nuclear war — can lead only to such complete destruction that, in the final analysis, the war will not have been worth fighting. This paradox provides the challenge and the setting for consideration of the role of military strategy in the nuclear age.

CHAPTER TWO

WARFARE IN THE NUCLEAR AGE

Changes in military technology and the subsequent impact of these changes on international politics have aroused much attention, particularly among students of international politics. This interest has produced new terminology and new concepts that help explain the role of military power in the nuclear age.

The most pervasive notion is that of "deterrence": that the primary function of military force should be to prevent the use of military force by one's opponents. The great destructive power of nuclear weapons has forced students of international politics to take more seriously the possibility of eliminating or substantially reducing the likelihood of war and, in particular, of large-scale thermonuclear war. The recognition that conflict is likely to remain a part of the international political scene, coupled with the belief that thermonuclear war would be so devastating as to be unacceptable, has led to the development of a typology of warfare and to an emphasis on the possibilities and problems of limiting war.

The first attempt to categorize wars came with the distinction between "limited" wars and "total" wars. A *limited war* was viewed as a conflict that would not involve the homelands of the United

States or the Soviet Union and that would be limited both in objectives and in the means used. A *total war* was a war involving attacks on the homelands of the United States and the Soviet Union. It was assumed that in such a war there would be no limit on either objectives or the means employed.

Recently analysts have felt the need to use the terms "general" and "local" to distinguish wars. A *general war* is a war involving attacks by the United States and the Soviet Union on each other's homelands. A *local war* is a war in which the United States and the Soviet Union see themselves on opposite sides but in which no attacks are made on the homelands of the two superpowers. Both a local war and a general war could be a "limited" war — limited in objectives or in the means used and targets attacked.

General War

Beginning about 1964, the world finally entered the missile age that had been heralded at least since 1957. By the middle of the 1960's the major strategic offensive nuclear forces of the United States and the Soviet Union were ballistic missiles. Missiles had become part of the arsenals of both countries in the late 1950's, but until the mid-1960's the airplane remained the dominant mode for delivery of nuclear weapons. The smaller payload of missiles and their potential for greater control over operations have raised the possibility of controlling a general nuclear war, should one occur. Analysis of the possibilities for limitation in general nuclear war suggests three kinds of wars involving the use of strategic attacks on the homelands of the United States and the Soviet Union.

Spasm War. Throughout the 1950's American statements and planning seemed to be based upon the assumption that a general nuclear war between the United States and the Soviet Union would be an all-out, or "spasm," war. It was believed that a general nuclear war could not be limited, and thus if a general nuclear war was started, each side would fire all its nuclear weapons at the other side as quickly as possible in a spasm reaction to the beginning of war. In such a war each side would presumably fire all its strategic forces at military and population targets in the other's homeland. In fact, the Soviet Union continues to talk publicly about general nuclear war in spasm-war terms.

Controlled Response. If one recognizes that the all-out, uncontrolled use of nuclear weapons by both superpowers would lead to substantial destruction of the population and industry of the two countries, then clearly both sides might attempt to limit a general nuclear war, should one take place. Even a large-scale nuclear war might be limited in terms of the targets attacked: each side might refrain from bombing the other's major cities and might concentrate instead on military targets. In addition, each side might not use all its strategic forces, holding some in reserve to threaten the destruction of its opponent's cities. However unlikely such restraints would be in the event of nuclear war, both the United States and the Soviet Union have taken such possibilities into account in designing their forces.

Limited Strategic Strikes. At the opposite extreme from spasm war is the proposal that strategic nuclear weapons be used in limited numbers. The possibilities of this kind of war range from the bizarre notion of one side's destroying one or several of its opponent's cities to the somewhat more likely possibility of engaging in limited strategic strikes at military or industrial targets far from the centers of population. Such strikes might be used either to influence the course of a local war that is in progress or to demonstrate a willingness to go to large-scale general nuclear war if necessary.

Motivations for War Initiation. A general nuclear war may be a *deliberate war* — that is, a war consciously and deliberately initiated by one of the two superpowers while that superpower is fully cognizant of its option to avoid such a war. Without being able to rule out entirely the possibility of a deliberate nuclear war, most analysts contend that *inadvertent war* is more likely, given the relative destruction that would occur to both countries. An inadvertent war would occur because one or both sides come to the conclusion that whatever the intentions of the two superpowers, general nuclear war has for some reason become inevitable. In this situation, the leadership that begins the war does so believing that the choice is not between general nuclear war or no general nuclear war but rather between general nuclear war that it has initiated or general nuclear war initiated by its adversary. In this situation the motive for war is simply the belief that war will occur and that it is better to strike first or at least be a close, rather than a distant, second.

Triggers of Nuclear War. The destructive power of nuclear weapons and the inability of the bureaucracy in the United States or the Soviet Union to guarantee to the top leadership that destruction would be kept to tolerable levels, even with a first strike, has minimized the probability of a deliberately initiated general nuclear war. However, there are certain situations in which one side or the other might be tempted to launch a deliberate strike.

If one of the superpowers believed it could escape substantial retaliation because of a lack of diligence on the part of its opponent in developing strategic systems capable of surviving an attack and penetrating active defenses, it might be tempted to launch a strike. However, even if calculation suggested that there would not be substantial retaliation, political leaders might find it difficult to believe the calculations. And even if they believed them, they would not necessarily decide to begin war. In the late 1940's the United States had a monopoly that would have enabled it to strike the Soviet Union with nuclear weapons without fear of retaliation. Although it is possible that, in the same position, the Soviet Union would not pass up such an opportunity, it is perhaps more likely that it would attempt to exploit the situation for political purposes rather than actually carry out a deliberate nuclear strike. Nevertheless, while analysts assert that the probability of a deliberate nuclear strike is extremely low, governments on both sides have felt obliged to spend a great deal of money and devote a lot of time to making sure that their opponent will never come to the conclusion that a successful first strike is possible.

A deliberate strike might also be carried out if the leadership in one country believed that the consequences of not starting a nuclear war were even more devastating than the outcome of a nuclear war. For example, the Soviet leaders *might* resort to all-out nuclear war if Communist control of Eastern Europe appeared to be threatened and if they believed that there was no other way of preventing the establishment of regimes friendly to the West. During the Cuban missile crisis of 1962, the United States threatened to initiate a general war if the Soviet Union or Cuba fired from Cuban territory a single missile that landed anywhere in the Western Hemisphere.

Finally, at least in principle, one cannot rule out complete irrationality — that is, a decision to launch general nuclear war for reasons unrelated to the direct consequences of the outcome of the war, perhaps involving personal, psychological impulses. The governments of both the United States and the Soviet Union have taken steps to ensure that irrational action below the top level of government could not lead to a general war. Though it is difficult to evaluate the effectiveness of these steps, they appear to be reliable and to reduce to the barest minimum the possibility of a war triggered by the irrationality of a subordinate. Irrationality of the top leadership is, of course, more difficult to prevent by formal institutional means, and it should not be forgotten that Stalin demonstrated some tendencies of a mentally unbalanced person, although probably not those that might have led him to launch a general nuclear war.

Much more likely than the triggering of a deliberate nuclear war is the triggering of an inadvertent general nuclear war. However, the two dangers interact with each other: the higher the probability of a deliberate attack, the greater the danger of an inadvertent general nuclear war. In order for an inadvertent war to take place, there must be, first, a belief in the high probability of war and, second, a perceived value of striking first if war occurs. A reduction in either of these would substantially reduce the possibility of a general nuclear war.

The perception that general nuclear war is impending depends on, in turn, a conducive setting and some triggering event. Neither the leadership of the United States nor that of the Soviet Union is likely to conclude in a period of international calm that the probability of general nuclear war is so high that it is necessary to strike first. Only during an intense political crisis, as has occurred from time to time over Berlin and over Cuba, or in a setting of local war, as in Korea and Indochina, might the superpowers be inclined to feel that a general nuclear war is imminent. The triggering event that then precipitates the general nuclear war may be one of several incidents. It may literally be an accident — that is, the detonation of a nuclear weapon or the firing of a missile because of mechanical or human failure. Another possibility — although remote — is an attempt by a country other than the United States or the Soviet Union to simulate the beginning of a nuclear war, perhaps by exploding a nuclear device. Finally, the trigger may simply come from the expansion of the local war or crisis: the war may become so intense that one side resorts to general nuclear war.

Even if the probability of general nuclear war seems high, the occurrence of an inadvertent war depends on the perception of a great value in striking first should war occur. During the early 1960's the world passed through a period in which both sides appeared to believe that in the event of nuclear war, there was a high value in striking first. This was partly because neither side had paid sufficient attention to developing forces able to survive a first strike but also because, in the period of transition from airplanes to missiles, a small number of missiles seemed capable of destroying a large number of airplanes in a surprise first strike.

During the 1960's first the United States and then the Soviet Union paid greater attention to the *vulnerability* of strategic forces to a surprise first strike. Both sides have developed relatively invulnerable forces — that is, forces difficult to destroy in a first strike and designed to ride out the first strike of the opponent. This relative invulnerability is developed in three ways: concealment, hardening, and mobility. The Soviets relied for several years on concealment of the location of their strategic forces. However, improvements in intelligence capacities, particularly satellites, rendered this method of developing relative invulerability comparatively ineffective. American *Minuteman* missiles and the newer Soviet ICBMs are in hardened underground sites protected by concrete silos. Mobility gives relative invulnerability to the American and Soviet missile-firing submarines, which keep in constant motion under the vast oceans. As strategic forces have become relatively invulnerable, the United States at least has come to the conclusion that if it is confronted with a Soviet first strike, it should not launch its weapons until after a significant number of Soviet missiles have landed on American territory. The United States has tried to make it clear to the Soviet Union that it has adopted this position, which should substantially reduce the probability of an inadvertent general nuclear war launched by either power. By removing fear of an American inadvertent strike, the Soviet need to strike first should be diminished. The United States has also stated that its policy is not to seek the capability of destroying Soviet strategic forces.

Despite the intensive efforts of both sides to develop invulnerable forces, technology in the early 1970's created the danger that the incentive to strike first would reappear. The deployment of highly accurate MIRVs, which would enable one missile to destroy several opposing missiles on the ground, coupled with large ABM systems, could by the late 1970's generate renewed fears of preemptive attack.

Local War

Analysts have attempted to distinguish general strategic nuclear war from local war. A local nuclear war is by definition limited in that it excludes the homelands of the two superpowers. However, a number of other limits have been observed in local wars that have taken place in the postwar period. It is important to remember that although analyses of general nuclear war must proceed simply on the basis of theoretical analysis, discussion of local non-nuclear war can draw on relevant historical examples as well as on theory.

If we look at the history of local war since World War II, we discover four limitations that have apparently been of great importance in keeping a local war from becoming a general nuclear war. The first of these involves the geography of the area in which the fighting is taking place. Not only have the homelands of the two superpowers been spared in all warfare, but so has much of the rest of the world. Each of the local wars that has taken place has been confined to a relatively small geographic area: the Taiwan Straits, Korea, Indochina, Cuba and its surrounding waters, and others.

Perhaps the most important limit that has been observed in local war in the postwar period has been the reluctance to use nuclear weapons. Neither of the two superpowers, when engaged in military action, has employed those weapons that, even at the tactical level, are judged to be most effective.

Another limitation observed in many local wars but violated or ignored by the United States in Cuba and more recently in Vietnam is the sanctity of supply lines beyond the area of battle. American action in Cuba was spectacular in that the United States sought for the first time since World War II to interfere with the movement of materiel into the area of potential conflict. Later in Vietnam the United States again ignored the "sanctuary" of North Vietnam and began to destroy supply lines moving into the area of battle and in 1970 moved against the enemy supply lines in Cambodia. However, even at the height of United States bombing raids on North Vietnam some limits were observed. The port of Haiphong was not mined and rail lines to China were not bombed.

The fourth major limitation is the level of participation of various countries in the local war. The two superpowers and China have been concerned with avoiding a direct confrontation of the troops of two of these countries. There has, of course, not been any direct confrontation of Soviet and American formal military forces.

Even in Korea, where American and Chinese troops clashed, American troops were disguised as part of a United Nations command and Chinese troops as volunteers. American actions in Vietnam in the 1960's demonstrate clearly the spectrum of roles that a superpower can play in relation to a local war. The United States began the decade providing diplomatic and economic support for the government of South Vietnam. It moved from that to providing military equipment and limited amounts of training on the ground in South Vietnam through a series of other steps leading up to the use of American combat troops. In 1968 the United States began to reverse the process.

How important the territory being fought over is to the superpowers is another key factor in determining the outcome and consequences of a local war. Some territories are more important to one of the superpowers than to the other. For example, the United States recognized the greater Soviet interest in Hungary and Czechoslovakia and greater Chinese interest in Tibet, while the Soviets, at least in the end, recognized the greater American interest in Cuba.

Although the interests and intentions of the superpowers are likely to be important determinants of the outcome of any local conflict, of equal or perhaps greater importance will be the local situation and the local political and military balance. Some wars, of course, start and end because of local conditions, and the superpowers never become involved. Even wars that turn out to be major confrontations between the United States, China, and the Soviet Union frequently begin because of local conditions and local pressures. The various conflicts in Vietnam and Laos, for example, were the result of pressures within Vietnam — some of them emanating from Indochinese Communists, but others, such as conflicts in Laos in 1962–1963, apparently resulting from the restlessness of neutralists under the leadership of Captain Kong Le. Other local conflicts erupt from the deliberate decision of leaders in Peking or Moscow. This appears to have happened in the Korean War and in various crises in the Taiwan Straits. Finally, we cannot exclude the possibility of the launching of a local war by the United States or another Western power, as was the case in the Suez crisis of 1956 and the Bay of Pigs invasion of Cuba in 1962

We are concerned about local wars partly because the outcomes of these wars may have important consequences for the future of international politics but also because of the possibility that a local war may turn into a general nuclear war. The word frequently used to express this danger is "escalation," which has now "escalated" into everyday vocabulary from the more technical vocabulary of the strategic analyst. Notice, however, that "escalation" is ambiguous and refers actually to two different processes that may come about as a local war grows in size. The first of these, *explosion,* involves the sudden occurrence of general nuclear war during the local war. This explosion into general nuclear war can take place at any time during a local war situation, even if the local war appears to be at a low level. However, it is more likely to occur after *expansion* (the second process implied by "escalation") of the local war — that is, the growth in size of a local war. Expansion may be deplored or applauded precisely because it increases the danger of general nuclear war: one side may want to show its determination by engaging in action that consequently increases the risk of an explosion into general war. An expansion of a local war may also be aimed at influencing the outcome of a local military battle.

Major Military Problems

The major military problems facing the United States may be considered as deterring and fighting a general nuclear war and deterring and fighting in local areas. Any military strategy dealing with any specific policy problem can be considered in terms of three components:

1. *Capability:* what hardware of various kinds — what missiles and airplanes, for example — a country should buy, with what

characteristics, how many of them with what air bases, what systems for communicating with military forces, and so on.

2. *Communication:* what it is that the leadership of a country wants its enemy to believe about how it will use the forces it has deployed. There is much less control over communications than over capabilities; however, the leadership of any country can, and frequently does, have an explicit policy of what it wants the enemy to believe. How to make the enemy believe this, amid much conflicting information from other sources both within the country and outside it, is a complex policy problem. In addition to what the leadership of a country says, the capabilities of a country, as well as its past and present action, influence the credibility to the enemy of that country's intentions.

3. *Action:* the actual plans for employing the military capability in any circumstances. In attempting to evaluate a historical strategy, we can identify the action policy of a country; looking to the future, we can only talk about what leaders of a country think they will do in a given situation.

Any government will be divided about what capabilities to buy, what signals to communicate, and what actions it should take. Its decisions will be a compromise of various positions, and its conduct will only in part be posed on high-level decisions. Nonetheless it is useful to examine the components of various possible strategies to understand their basic structure and purpose.

General Nuclear War

Five alternative strategies for deterring or fighting a general nuclear war can be identified. Two of these strategies, *minimum deterrence* and *credible first strike,* have advocates outside the government but have never been seriously considered by the American government. The other three strategies are variations of the strategy of *assured destruction,* which has formed the basis of American policy during the postwar period.

When a country employs a strategy of minimum deterrence, it

uses a relatively small strategic force to attack enemy population centers in order to convince the enemy that it will only use the force in retaliation for an enemy first strike. The strategic forces are used, if at all, in a second strike; little concern is given to the actual fighting of a general nuclear war.

The strategy of a credible first strike calls for the development of a large strategic offensive force — two or three times more than that called for by an assured destruction strategy — capable of destroying most of the enemy's strategic forces. It also requires a large ABM system designed to shoot down enemy missiles that survive a first strike. By using the strategy of a credible first strike, a country would convey to its enemy that there is a significant probability that a first strike will be launched in the event of various kinds of provocation. In the event of war, this strategy prescribes a large first strike directed at all the enemy's strategic forces.

Assured deterrence strategies rest on the basic assumption that what is necessary to deter a nuclear war is the ability without question to destroy the enemy society after receiving an all-out attack. The variations in the strategy depend on two questions of capability: (1) how much force is necessary to deter and (2) whether some additional capability to seek to limit damage in the event of war should be purchased. The effort in employing this strategy is to convince the potential enemy that one is not threatening his deterrent by developing a first strike capability and that in the event of nuclear war both countries will be destroyed. In the event of war an effort would be made to use nuclear forces in a controlled way but with little expectation that a nuclear war could be limited.

These alternatives raise a number of specific issues, which can be considered in terms of capability, communication, and action.

A major issue of American defense policy in the postwar period has been how much of a strategic force is enough. Or, as the critics of current policy put it: How much "overkill" do we need? The answer to this question depends on a judgment about how much is necessary to deter an attack and whether nuclear forces should be brought for other purposes — for example, to try to limit damage in the event of war. Some analysts have suggested that a small strategic force, perhaps one hundred intercontinental missiles, is sufficient; at the other extreme, some have argued that the United States should produce as many strategic forces as it can. The decisions in between are much more complicated. Most analysts now accept that Soviet forces are so large that it is not feasible for the United States to prevent the Soviet Union from inflicting massive damage on American cities in the event of nuclear war. Thus the recent debate has largely centered on how much is enough to deter.

Just as important as the quantity of the strategic forces is the quality of those forces: their accuracy and their ability to survive an enemy attack, to penetrate enemy defenses, and to be used in controlled and sophisticated ways. During the 1960's the United States — and apparently to some extent the Soviet Union — spent large sums of money improving the quality of strategic forces, in particular, command and control systems and the ability to use the force.

American communication policy about general nuclear war has been ambiguous throughout the postwar period. On the one hand, American officials emphasize the traditional American reluctance to begin a general nuclear war and state that the United States would never be the "aggressor." On the other hand, it is clear that American policy for the defense of Europe includes the threat to launch a nuclear attack on the Soviet Union in response to a Soviet attack in Europe.

A second major issue in communications has been what sort of attack the United States should threaten to launch. Should the United States indicate that it will bomb cities as well as strategic forces? The United States has stated that it might not strike Soviet cities, particularly if the Soviet Union refrained from attacking American cities. Soviet statements, on the other hand, have implied that cities as well as strategic forces would be struck in the event of a nuclear war.

Deterrence of a deliberate attack would appear to be strengthened by emphasis on the hair-trigger nature of, or loosely controlled, strategic forces, because if strategic forces are only loosely controlled, they can more readily react to early signs of an enemy attack and, consequently, are less likely to be destroyed. On the contrary, however, American communication policy has stressed that American strategic forces are under tight command and control, would not be used in provocative ways, and would not be launched until after a number of Soviet missiles had exploded in the United States.

Since the development of an American atomic arsenal, military planners have produced plans for the employment of nuclear weapons, should they be ordered into use by the President. There has been considerable reluctance in the United States and elsewhere to think about what would occur in the event of general nuclear war.

A major question, which now appears to have been answered, is whether the United States should contemplate preemptive nuclear war. American leaders apparently have enough confidence in the ability of United States strategic forces to survive a Soviet first strike that they are determined to be sure that the strike has occurred, by waiting for a significant number of missiles to hit the United States, before launching American forces. In this way American forces would not be triggered by "geese on the radar screen," the accidental firing of a few Soviet missiles, or an attempt by a local Soviet commander or a third country to simulate an all-out Soviet attack. Although the United States has retained the option of striking first in response to massive Soviet aggression in Europe, it has emphasized the desire not to be faced by this dilemma by increasing its own ability to respond to Soviet aggression in kind or at levels below a general nuclear strike.

Perhaps the most significant question that would face the United States in the event of a nuclear war would be how large a strike to employ. If American action were in response to a Soviet strike, the magnitude of the strike would very likely be influenced by the nature of the Soviet attack. At one extreme, the United States might launch all its strategic forces against military targets and population centers in the Soviet Union. At the other extreme, it would launch a limited strike against a few targets in the Soviet Union, withholding the great bulk of its force to threaten city destruction. In the 1950's American strategy seemed to call for the destruction of Soviet cities as quickly as possible in the event of war. From this perspective one talked about the "bonus damage" received from attacking strategic targets: the United States would get added value from an attack in which a weapon that struck an airbase would through its fallout or blast kill a large number of civilians, for destruction in the Soviet Union would be increased. Another approach to city damage is essentially to ignore it — that is, to launch strategic forces against Soviet military installations without reference to whether this brings on large-scale civilian destruction — neither desiring civilian destruction nor taking any steps to avoid it. A third approach suggests launching a sizable attack against strategic forces but avoiding city damage.

The withholding of strategic forces that could be used in city destruction rests on the belief that deterrence can continue even after general nuclear war begins. It is assumed that there will be communication, perhaps on the so-called hot line between Moscow and Washington, and also that both sides will communicate by the way in which they use their strategic forces. Because we need to communicate only if we want to negotiate an end to the war, communication would suggest willingness to stop the war short of the all-out use of strategic forces, combined with a threat to attack cities if the war continues. The problem of how to terminate a general nuclear war is one that has been given little attention in the United States.

The Defense of Local Areas

The deterrence of general nuclear war has received the most attention in the United States not because such war has been viewed as the most likely military threat, but rather because it is seen as the most serious threat — one that could cause destruction of American civilization. However, local threats are much more likely. Such threats have taken in the past, and could in the future take, three forms: nuclear blackmail, conventional attack, and subversion.

In trying to deal with threats of local aggression, the United States has at least in principle a series of options. First, it can hope that local forces themselves will be sufficient to deal with the threat. Second, it can depend on its own or alliance ground forces. Finally, it can try to use strategic nuclear forces.

The causes of local aggression are many. Because of this, and because in many areas of the world no acceptable substitute for violence as a means of political change has developed, much more attention has been given to actually fighting than to simply deterring local wars. A variety of strategies has been proposed for this purpose, mainly with reference to meeting American treaty commitments in Europe and in East Asia. The alternatives that have been suggested are massive retaliation, limited retaliation, the use of alliance strategic nuclear forces, the use of national strategic nuclear forces, and direct defense with or without nuclear weapons.

The strategy of massive retaliation holds that forces sufficient to deter a Soviet nuclear strike on the United States are sufficient to deter or defeat any lesser aggression. The strategy suggests that the United States needs little beyond its strategic nuclear capabilities and that it should threaten to conduct a first strike in the event of aggression. This capability is viewed as adequate to deter any Soviet or Chinese move. It calls for a credible first strike capability.

A second strategy, which depends at least in part on the use of strategic forces, is that of limited retaliation. It is the policy implied by Secretary of State Dulles in his famous "massive retaliation" speech. This strategy calls for the limited use of strategic forces to deter or defeat local aggression and proposes that the United States communicate to its opponents that it will not deal with aggression on the level on which it occurs but rather will feel free to respond with nuclear weapons against strategic targets in the homeland of China or of the Soviet Union.

The strategies of massive and limited retaliation are based on the employment of American strategic forces. Both of these lines of action might also be implemented by alliance nuclear forces or by the national nuclear forces possessed by the country attacked.

Strategies that employ strategic forces — whether controlled by the United States or its allies — to defend local areas against direct attack also call for some ground forces to establish the fact that aggression has taken place. The enemy would have to attack and destroy the existing ground forces, leaving no doubt that aggression had occurred. The limits of the use of strategic nuclear forces in deterring various kinds of aggression, particularly those involving political pressure or guerrilla warfare, have become increasingly evident, and attention has been focused on direct defense. The three central questions that arise here are: How large should American General Purpose Forces — forces designed for defense of local areas — be? Should the United States commit its own forces or rely on indigenous forces? Should the United States use a tactical nuclear weapon strategy or a conventional strategy in the defense of particular areas?

The main capability problems are: (1) how large United States General Purpose Forces should be, (2) what forces should be procured, and (3) what forces should be deployed overseas. General Purpose Forces account for almost 50 per cent of the American defense budget. As many critics have sought ways to reduce defense spending, they have come to focus on the General Purpose Forces. One major issue is how many contingencies American armed forces should be prepared to engage in simultaneously. During the 1960's, planning was based on what came to be called the 2½ war concept; the United States tried to be ready to fight at the same time a large war in Europe, a large war in Asia, and a minor contingency elsewhere. To meet this objective the size of American ground forces was substantially increased from 13 to 18⅓ divisions. President Nixon directed a change in planning to prepare for what he called a 1½ war concept, and the United States now prepares to engage in a large war either in Asia or in Europe while supporting Asian allies and engaging in a minor contingency. Determining the number of contingencies provides only a general guide to what capability is needed. Specific questions concerning, for example, how many aircraft carriers should be deployed and what tactical fighter aircraft the Air Force and Navy should buy are difficult to answer and depend on a complex analysis of risks. Judging how much to spend on these forces also requires weighing domestic against foreign priorities.

Questions about the location of American forces center around whether the United States should continue to maintain approximately five divisions in Europe and two divisions in South Korea as well as the extensive American base structure in East Asia. Answers depend in part on an assessment of the political role of overseas forces and their value for deterrence as well as on the ability of the United States to redeploy forces rapidly by using its extensive airlift and sealift capacity.

Communication policy for a local war is exceedingly difficult to specify in the abstract. The United States has been faced with the problem in several locations and has had to decide whether to threaten intervention and, if so, how ambiguous to be about the threat. Another question has been whether to threaten intervention with or without the use of nuclear weapons. The same problems exist with determining action policies: When should the United States intervene and when should it use nuclear weapons?

It should be clear that the creation of modern weapons has posed a series of formidable and novel problems both for the strategic analyst and for American and Soviet policymakers. Considerable effort has been given to developing techniques, particularly quantitative ones, for dealing with these problems.

CHAPTER THREE

QUANTITATIVE AND QUALITATIVE RESEARCH METHODS

Military strategy may be viewed as an aspect of the role of force in international politics. However, strategic questions have also been studied in the postwar period from several other perspectives. A policy perspective has been adopted within the government and also in private research institutes such as the RAND Corporation. Should the United States deploy medium-range missiles in Europe? What threats should have been made during the Cuban missile crisis? What action should have been taken during the Berlin blockade? Questions of policy such as these have been subjected to systematic analysis.

Others have seen military strategy as an aspect of a broader theoretical interest. For example, for some economists, military-strategy decisions are part of the problem of the allocation of scarce resources. For some game theorists (those who study the mathematical theory of games) military strategy has proven to be a fertile field for examples of competitive and cooperative interaction. Others with a general interest in "conflict" theory have looked to military questions for insights and applications.

This chapter will examine *quantitative methods* — that is, the use of mathematics and statistics — that have been used in the study of military strategy, assess their limitations, and explore ways in which quantitative methods can be combined with *qualitative methods* — those not using numbers.

Quantitative Methods

Two basic quantitative methods have been introduced into the study of military strategy. Within the framework of these two methods a number of specific quantitative techniques have been suggested. The first method is *systems analysis:* an attempt to assess the effectiveness of a military weapon as a complete system in operation over a period of time against an opponent who calculates what his enemy may do. The techniques of systems analysis are used, for example, to calculate the possible outcome of a general nuclear war and to assess the effect on the likely outcome of the war of new weapon systems or new strategies used in existing systems. One systems study done for the government on a classified basis in the early 1950's and publicly released in the 1960's examined the role of overseas bases in American strategic foreign policy. It drew on a variety of quantitative techniques to assess the most efficient way of using existing American bombers and those to be procured. The study examined possible combinations of American and overseas bases and recommended optimum deployment of planes on bases. Systems-analysis studies relate to situations in which there are competing objectives. Where there is only one objective — for example, to destroy enemy submarines — operations analysis is used.

The second method — one frequently used in conjunction with systems analysis — is *cost-effectiveness comparative analysis.* It seeks to compare the cost of using two different methods to secure a particular objective or, alternatively, the relative effectiveness of two systems having approximately the same cost. This technique involves looking not only at the cost of buying particular hardware but also at the five-year operating cost of the military equipment being purchased. This method frequently uses concepts from economics, such as marginal utility.

The techniques of systems analysis and cost effectiveness have been used increasingly in the Pentagon since Robert S. McNamara became the Secretary of Defense in 1961. His successors, Clark Clifford and Melvin Laird, continued to use quantitative analyses although they relied less heavily on them. Much of this analysis is classified, but there are some unclassified studies. By examining one major quantitative issue, we should be able to understand the quantification techniques and also the value of using them — even if only with illustrative numbers — to comprehend the problem. Relatively accurate data for quantitative analysis can be obtained from unclassified sources.

Quantitative studies of a recent controversial issue can illustrate both the utility of systems-analysis and cost-effectiveness studies and their sensitivity to assumptions made about how the systems will perform. In 1969 President Nixon announced a reorientation of the proposed ABM system so that its primary purpose would be the defense of American missiles against a Soviet attack aimed at destroying them in a first strike. This decision was based on calculations that, if the Soviets deployed 500 SS-9 intercontinental missiles with 3 MIRVs each of five megatons, 95 per cent of the American *Minuteman* force could be destroyed. Critics suggested that, if slightly different assumptions were made, 25 per cent of the force would survive. The different percentages were due to varying estimates of the hardness of American missiles and the accuracy and reliability of Soviet missiles. An important question was whether the Soviets could get information about missiles that had malfunctioned and then retarget a second missile against the designated target.

Qualitative Methods

Even the most enthusiastic advocates of quantitative methods warn that these methods must be combined with qualitative insights in making strategic decisions. However, because of the amorphous nature of qualitative inputs, the need to add them to quantitative analysis is frequently overlooked. In fact, it is difficult to specify the nature of the techniques used in qualitative analysis. They involve using the lessons one has learned from history, from a general study of politics, and from a particular study of the enemies and allies with which one is dealing. But how these insights are to be used seems to defy organized analysis.

In addition to its direct role in dealing with strategic issues, qualitative analysis is important in specifying the terms for any quantitative analysis. For example, systems analysts frequently stress the great importance of asking the right questions of the data being analyzed. Consideration of the vulnerability of strategic forces to destruction on the ground by the enemy, of the cost to the enemy of countering any action taken by its opponent, and of the five-year operating costs as well as the purchase costs of any given military equipment — these qualitative insights have drastically altered the shape of all quantitative analysis done on strategic problems in the United States in recent years. Insights of this kind can arise not only from qualitative analysis but also in the process of carrying out quantitative analysis — a fact that underlines the value of even heuristic exercises.

The Interaction of Quantitative and Qualitative Analyses

There is little dispute that one needs to use quantitative data wherever possible, but there is also no question that if one goes beyond narrow technical questions, quantitative data alone are not sufficient. Several interactions between qualitative and quantitative analyses in capability, communication, and action illustrate the process of strategic analysis.

The question of determining the optimum military capability for the United States, with a given defense budget, is in one sense a problem in the economic analysis of scarce resources. In another sense, it is a problem of dealing with a rational and responsive opponent. Three different issues, which have been important in American defense policy in the postwar period, will be considered in order to illustrate the roles of qualitative and quantitative analyses in the assessment of decisions about military capability.

The first of these issues is the role of strategic forces. Part of making decisions is asking the right questions — that is, developing the right qualitative insights about what the issues really are. One essential question is: How vulnerable are various systems to an enemy strategic first strike? Another seeks the goals desired from using strategic forces: Is deterrence alone the goal? Is limiting damage, if war occurs, a concern? Is it possible to win the war in some sense? Finally, are strategic forces to be used for purposes other than deterring or fighting a general nuclear war? In order to answer such questions, we need detailed quantitative analyses of the costs of accomplishing various objectives. Systems analyses combining the operation of a variety of strategic offensive and defensive systems are required. The cost of obtaining a certain probability of destroying a given target is a valid concern; so is the decrease in casualties in the United States if the Soviet Union can be induced not to attack American cities.

Thus quantitative analysis is important and necessary but does not come close to providing a complete answer. What we need to know is the enemy's calculation — not our own calculations — of under what circumstances he will attack, for his calculations may be different for a variety of reasons. Thus, if we are most interested in strategic forces because of their role in deterring the enemy's use of strategic forces, our most important calculations will be what, in fact, will deter the enemy; this is not necessarily the same as what will actually work most effectively should a war occur.

In addition, in determining the role of strategic forces, we are likely to discover important conflicts between various values. For example, one strategic posture may look best in terms of deterring an inadvertent attack, another most efficient in terms of deterring a deliberate attack, and a third most effective in limiting damage should war occur. Conflicts may also arise between objectives of strategic weapons and other objectives in, as well as outside, the defense field. Even if we could determine exactly how much deterrence we could buy for a given sum of money, the question of whether that much deterrence is worth buying could be judged only in relation to what else we could buy with that money. Finally, the domestic, political, and social costs of any strategic posture must be assessed.

At the highest level of generalization, quantitative analysis is extremely complicated and difficult to perform; it plays a vital but limited role in strategic analysis. However, the more limited the decisions are, the greater the role of quantitative methods.

A limited decision about military capability would be whether the United States should buy a new bomber. The role of quantitative analysis in solving this problem is greater than in evaluating the role of strategic forces. The question is primarily one of cost effectiveness: comparing any new manned bomber with other systems in relation to their ability both to limit damage if war should occur and to deter a nuclear war in the context of any given strategy.

The first objective — limiting damage if war occurs — is a straightforward quantitative problem, except for uncertainties such as how good the enemy defense is and how well the pilot can fly. Given the goal of reducing damage in a certain kind of general nuclear war, the relative effectiveness of a particular bomber, as opposed to other strategic systems, is easy to determine.

The deterrent role of bombers, on the other hand, is more difficult to determine. It is impossible to quantify the role of bombers in deterrence beyond restating the cost effectiveness of the bombers. However, the more relevant calculation may be the enemy's estimate of cost effectiveness and beyond that the psychological impact of the existence or absence of bombers in the American strategic force.

Finally, other priorities within the American economy — for example, dealing with urgent domestic problems and reducing draft calls — can, and legitimately do, come into play in deciding whether to produce any given weapon system.

The third illustration of a capability decision is a local-war problem; it poses the question of how to spend funds efficiently for

American ground troops. For a variety of historical reasons — including the fact that the RAND Corporation, which has been the pioneer in developing quantitative techniques, has done most of its work for the Air Force — there has been relatively little quantitative work on local-war problems. Moreover, such problems are not too susceptible to systematic quantitative analysis. There are, however, three alternatives, which could be used in combination, for deploying military forces so that they would be effective in any particular spot on the globe. The first alternative is to keep all forces and their equipment in the United States and spend large sums of money on airlift and sealift capability. At the other extreme is the second alternative: to try to station the forces in the area in which military conflict is anticipated. A third alternative is to position heavy equipment in the areas of likely conflict and to station the troops and their light equipment, with extensive airlift capability, in the United States.

Clearly, there are important quantitative aspects to this problem. In one sense, it is simply a problem of operations analysis — that is, systems analysis in which there are no conflicting objectives — the only objective being to get the most men with a given combat efficiency to the most areas at the least cost. But considering, for example, the real issue of decreasing the number of American troops stationed in Europe and, instead, positioning equipment in Europe, with increased airlift capabilities for forces stationed in the United States, we realize that political considerations — which cannot be quantified — can dominate the problem. In this case, perhaps the most important political consideration is the German belief that the more American troops there are in Europe, the more likely it is that the United States will fight to defend West Germany.

The deterrence of local war is perhaps even more complicated than the deterrence of a Soviet nuclear strike. Again we have to deal with both inadvertent and deliberate aggression and also with aggression from a variety of different parties and the possibility of a spontaneous outbreak of violence. It is almost impossible to specify, for the deterrence of any given action or possible combination of actions, the relative effectiveness of five divisions on the ground in Europe or two divisions and the equipment for three more divisions, which could be flown in within two weeks.

In the postwar period, the number of American ground troops in Europe has had a significant effect on alliance relations, and this effect has been an important factor in determining the number of ground troops to be maintained. The United States has kept a large army in Europe for the purpose of reinforcing the credibility that it will use its strategic nuclear forces — if necessary — to defeat Soviet aggression. During the early postwar period these forces also provided a suitable framework for an acceptable rearmament of West Germany; they are now important in demonstrating an American political commitment to Europe. None of these objectives is easy to quantify, and whatever qualifications would be involved would not be directly related to the military capability of the forces.*

Quantitative analysis is of important, but limited, value in the study of capability requirements, and it is of even less value in the study of communication and action policies. Perhaps the main role of quantitative analysis in devising an effective communication policy is determining the credibility of a statement.

To choose an example from the local-war area, there is much discussion about whether the United States should convince the Soviet Union that it is willing to fight a conventional war in Europe. There is an important quantitative issue here — namely, the cost of deploying conventional defense forces capable of defeating a Soviet conventional attack of a given magnitude. But many uncertainties exist both in the data and in the methods to be used. For example, the size of the Soviet force in Europe is not precisely known by intelligence specialists. Moreover, how to compute the effectiveness

* The behaviorally oriented political scientist will recognize that the focus of this chapter is on quantitative methods uniquely related to problems of military strategy. Many of the problems described here as "qualitative" could be subjected to at least partial quantitative analysis by techniques used by behavioral scientists.

of these ground forces and the likely outcome of a ground battle has not been determined.

All these questions are overshadowed in importance by one question: What actions are the NATO governments willing and able to take? If, for example, Europeans believe that an increase in conventional capability decreases deterrence and if they believe this because of judgments about Soviet attitudes, no amount of quantitative debate about the cost of the conventional capabilities will change their position. By the same token, if governments agree that conventional forces would improve deterrence but feel that the money is better spent on housing or world economic developments, the quantitative data is of limited value.

The debate about whether the United States should communicate to the Soviets that a nuclear war might be fought without attacking cities in the early stages of the war reveals the same relatively limited role for quantitative analysis. Here, again, there is an extremely important quantitative question: What would the decrease in casualties in the United States, the Soviet Union, and Western Europe be if attacks by both sides were directed at strategic targets only and not at cities? But we have to go beyond that question and ask questions about the effect of deterrence on the arms race and on alliance relationships — questions that so far have defied quantitative analysis.

When we turn to action policies, the complications in analysis become even more pronounced, and the emphasis has tended to be on providing the decision-maker with options and flexibility so that he can respond wisely to a variety of situations. However, it may become important in some situations to assess the probable outcome of a military conflict in order to determine the proper action policy.

Assessing the probable outcome was important during the Cuban missile crisis of 1962. One of the many questions facing American decision-makers at that time was how valuable missiles in Cuba would be to the Soviet Union in case of a war. Here the systems analysis was relatively complicated; it posed several different questions: Who would strike first, the Soviet Union or the United States? Would the war begin after an alert of the strategic forces? What was the cost and the feasibility of an airborne alert for bombers for the purpose of reducing their vulnerability to Soviet missiles in Cuba? By ignoring the great uncertainties involved, it was possible to produce quantitative answers about the effect on various war outcomes of Soviet placement of a given number of missiles in Cuba.

The effect on the course of international politics or even on the outcome of a general nuclear war was a much more difficult problem to analyze. For example, the calculations assumed that a war with strategic-force targets was relevant either because it might occur or because if it did occur it would affect political decisions. However, it is by no means clear that these assumptions were valid. Moreover, what appeared to be important were perceptions on both sides about how the Soviet move would change the strategic balance. Most political analysts — not to speak of politicians and the general public — tended to discuss this question in completely qualitative terms, arguing that Soviet missiles in Cuba would "drastically alter" or "tip" the strategic balance, and they tended to discount the quantitative factors. However, it is important to note that because a country is concerned with effects on other governments and other peoples, it does no good to say that these countries *should* take the *quantitative* factors into account: we must live with qualitative political judgments. In fact, perceptions of the effect on the strategic balance were less important than the United States image in Latin America, the likely Soviet moves in Berlin, and other political problems that may not have been closely related to the real military utility of deploying Soviet missiles in Cuba. As with each of the examples discussed in this chapter, quantitative calculations were important but provided only part of the answer to any real policy question.

CHAPTER FOUR

THE EVOLUTION OF AMERICAN MILITARY STRATEGY

American military strategy has evolved continuously over the postwar period in response to changes in technology as well as to increased sophistication in the understanding of strategic questions. This chapter will trace the evolution of American policy as well as the evolution of the analysis of strategic questions and will consider the role of technology in shaping these evolutions.

The Early Postwar Period

During the early postwar period the United States gradually came to accept the need for a policy to halt the spread of Soviet communism, which threatened to engulf all Europe. The Truman administration accepted the containment doctrine, which argued that if Soviet expansion could be stopped, the Soviet Union would gradually lose its urge to expand. The doctrine developed from an analysis of Soviet society, and the implications of this doctrine were viewed largely in political and economic terms. The military implications of an attempt to stop Soviet expansion and, consequently, the kind of military forces that might be needed over the next ten years were not given much attention.

Defense strategy in the early postwar period focused on the problem of general war, which was defined at that time as large-scale Soviet aggression in Europe. The possibility of limited local aggression, either in Europe or outside of it, was not taken seriously in war planning or force development. Very early in this period the concept of deterrence — that is, preventing a Soviet attack in Europe — became important. The main emphasis was on a political commitment by the United States to defend Europe; this commitment culminated in the signing of the NATO Defense Treaty in 1949. There was a widespread belief that the second (and even the first) world war had come about because aggressors had assumed that the United States would remain aloof and would permit them to dominate Europe. Thus it was argued that a firm commitment in the form of the North Atlantic Treaty would be a major step toward effectively deterring a Soviet attack. Although it was recognized that the atomic bomb might potentially change all military strategy, this bomb was viewed in the postwar period simply as a somewhat bigger bomb to be used in the same way other bombs had been used at the end of World War II. The United States had a small stockpile of atomic weapons, and there was no strong drive to increase to any great extent the size of the stockpile. Conventional forces were even smaller. The United States defense budget stood at approximately $15 billion a year, and a popular notion in Washington was that any sum larger than that would bankrupt the economy.

NSC 68 (1950)

By 1950 a number of pressures made a reevaluation of American defense policy in the atomic age a necessity. It had become clear that, because the cold war would last for a long time, the United States would continue to have defense commitments, which should be reevaluated in light of the growing American atomic stockpiles.

First, the Soviet Union had become a nuclear power much more quickly than anybody had expected, and the United States had decided to proceed on a top priority basis with the development of the hydrogen (fusion), or "super," bomb. This decision, made by President Truman, was one of the three immediate pressures that led to a review of American defense strategy. The second pressure came from the growing American military assistance program and the efforts of the State Department to coordinate defense and foreign policy. The tradition of separating foreign policy from military strategy made it difficult to devise an effective military assistance program; officials in the State Department, particularly Paul Nitze of the Policy Planning Staff, became aware of the need to coordinate defense and foreign policy. Finally, President Truman called on the National Security Council to take a more active role in coordinating security policy and asked the National Security Council for an appraisal of the United States strategic situation.

These pressures led to the creation of a joint State-Defense Department committee, which was instructed to reexamine American security policy without considering either budgetary or political constraints. The committee, with the strong support of Secretary of State Dean Acheson and the active guiding role of Nitze, met for several months during 1950 and finally reported to the National Security Council in April. The report, NSC 68, endorsed by both the State Department and the Defense Department, called for a substantial increase in the American defense effort and warned of the danger of local wars. President Truman indicated his intention to accept the report but asked for cost estimates. These were being prepared when the Korean War broke out, and NSC 68 served as a blueprint for actual rearmament.

The Korean War

The Korean War was accompanied by a vast increase in American defense spending. The defense budget went up rapidly and then leveled off at approximately $40 billion a year — almost three times the $15 billion ceiling that had been reaffirmed shortly before the war. Despite the attack in the Far East and the fighting in the Korean peninsula, the emphasis remained on Europe. It was believed that the Korean War might be a feint on the part of the Communists to draw American power into Asia while preparing for a Soviet move in Central Europe. Thus, while the Korean War was going on, the American forces in NATO were built up substantially. The decision was made to create the post of Supreme Allied Commander for Europe, and General Dwight D. Eisenhower was appointed to the position. In 1952 the NATO Council met in Lisbon and established goals for the buildup of NATO ground forces to a total of about seventy-five active and reserve divisions on the central front in Germany. The United States rapidly expanded its own nuclear and airpower capabilities. In defense planning during the Korean War, the United States adopted the notion of a "crisis year": several years in the future there would be a peak period of danger for the United States, and in order to prepare for war in that crisis year, excessive American defense expenditures were currently required.

The New Look

The Eisenhower administration came into office in 1953 committed not only to ending the Korean War but also to taking a "new look" at American military strategy. We can identify at least three major sources of the new approach of the administration.

The first of these was an affinity for airpower, which strangely enough influenced both President Eisenhower — a former Army general — and Admiral Arthur William Radford, who was to become Eisenhower's first chairman of the Joint Chiefs. The belief that airpower could be the backbone of the American military establishment stemmed from a notion that technology could somehow substitute for manpower. The United States, being short on manpower but highly advanced technologically, could be expected — it was argued — to find a solution to its military problems by relying on its strengths and de-emphasizing its weaknesses. In addition, the emphasis on airpower was a search for a single solution to a complex problem, a characteristic American approach.

Of perhaps equal importance in the search for a new strategy was the notion of the great equation: the belief that the security of the United States depended as much on the health of the American economy as it did on the actual weapons used in warfare and that this health resulted from keeping expenditures down. It was felt that a lower defense budget would in the long run contribute more to military security than a higher budget would.

Finally, an important technological innovation of the new strategy in the United States was the development of the so-called tactical nuclear weapons — nuclear weapons of low yield that might be used on the battlefield. Breakthroughs in technology and vast increases in the American stockpile of nuclear weapons made it possible to talk about such a use of nuclear weapons.

What, then, were the characteristics of this new look? First of all, the notion of a crisis year was discarded and was replaced by the "long haul" concept. The crisis-year notion had been used by the Truman administration to justify large expenditures on the grounds that they would level off and be reduced after the United States had passed the year of great crisis. The new long-haul concept, on the other hand, justified reduced expenditures on the grounds that they would be continued indefinitely. In addition, nuclear deterrence was given more attention than it had been given before. Under the Truman administration prior to, and during, the Korean War, the greatest threat was believed to be in Europe; it was felt that this threat was best deterred by political commitments and by nuclear power. With the advent of the new look, the dominant role of the Air Force in American strategy was formalized. From this followed a de-emphasis on ground forces — particularly on the possibility and desirability of a conventional defense. By 1954 the NATO Council had formally committed NATO to the use of tactical nuclear weapons in the event of large-scale fighting on the central front, and NATO force requirements were reduced in the belief that tactical nuclear weapons could substitute for manpower.

A comparison of the new look policy and the pre–Korean War policy of the Truman administration reveals innovations and similarities. In both periods, the need to keep the defense budget low in order to permit the growth and health of the economy was emphasized; deterrence was largely to come from the use of atomic or nuclear weapons. Nevertheless, articulation of the military doctrines inherent in United States policy since World War II resulted in a major critique of this policy, leading ultimately to its drastic revision.

Criticism of Massive Retaliation

In January 1954, Secretary of State John Foster Dulles made a speech attempting to explain and to justify the new look policy of the administration — particularly the administration's reluctance to engage in renewed ground combat in Asia. In his talk, Dulles declared that no local defense could contain the manpower of the Communist world; therefore, he said, local defense must be reinforced by the threatened deterrent of massive retaliatory power. The United States could deter local aggression by maintaining a great capacity to retaliate instantly "by means and in places of our own choosing." Dulles' formal statement of what in reality had long been the policy of the administration provoked a storm of criticism, not only from leading Democrats, but also from a number of students of national security policy. These critics, who included Chester Bowles and Dean Acheson, as well as such academics as William Kaufmann and Henry Kissinger, argued that the doctrine of massive retaliation would not be effective in deterring local, ambiguous Communist moves. They contended that massive retaliation could not be the action policy of the United States because to implement a doctrine of massive retaliation would be suicidal. Therefore, they concluded, a local-war strategy for the defense of areas outside of Europe was needed. At this stage, most critics of the massive-retaliation doctrine did not question its validity in Europe; only in the late 1950's and eary 1960's was it felt that a direct defense strategy was essential for Europe also.

Dulles' statement was not a major change in policy, certainly not from earlier formulations of the new look, and not even from the policy of the Truman administration. Neither was it clear that the policy should be interpreted — as its critics suggested — as a warning that the United States would bomb Moscow in the event of an attack by Communist forces anywhere in the world. On the contrary, the doctrine might well be interpreted as a form of limited retaliation: the United States would not necessarily meet ground action where it occurred but might respond — with or without nuclear weapons — with attacks on strategic targets, perhaps in the Soviet Union, perhaps only in China and other Communist states. There seems to be little doubt that the option of limited-retaliation and even massive-retaliation, strategy is desirable because it contributes to general deterrence, and it is now believed that Dulles' threats did enhance American deterrence of Chinese action in the Far East.

Moreover, the assumption implicit in most of the criticism was that the nuclear balance between the United States and the Soviet Union was inherently stable, that nuclear war was unlikely and was deterred simply by each side's having nuclear weapons. There was little regard for the vulnerability of these weapons to an enemy attack; rather, it was believed that nuclear war would consist primarily of attacks on cities. This image enabled Dulles' critics to say that if he was threatening Moscow, he had to accept in return the threat of New York's destruction. In fact, in 1954 and for several years after, both the United States and the Soviet Union could have destroyed, in a strategic first strike, much of their enemy's capacity to retaliate. It was not until still later that critics outside the government began to warn that the administration was not only overlooking the need for large ground forces but also the need for well-protected strategic forces.

Finally, it should be noted that at least some of the issues between Dulles and his critics were quantitative ones that had been expressed qualitatively. Dulles recognized and accepted the need for local-war forces; he argued, however, that by themselves they would never be large enough to contain communism and therefore had to be supplemented by nuclear power. His critics presumably were contending that larger forces could — and should — be supplied and that these forces might at least in some circumstances be sufficient to deter or defeat a Communist attack. The real issue, then, was the size of the American ground forces, not what they should be used for.

In the long run, the critics of the massive-retaliation doctrine made their impact on the intellectual climate and defense thinking in the United States. This influence culminated in 1961, when a number of these critics were brought into power with the Kennedy administration. Their effect on policy during the remaining years of the Eisenhower administration, however, was to be much less dramatic. The criticisms did slowly bring about a few changes, though. The need for larger ground forces — at least for tactical nuclear ground defense — was accepted. Finally, the need for a limited-war strategy — albeit a nuclear one — was acknowledged late in 1957, when the trend of thinking was suddenly reversed.

Sputnik *and the Gaither Committee*

In October 1957 the first artificial earth satellite — the Soviet *Sputnik* — was launched into the sky, creating the impression of Soviet superiority not only in technology but also in military capability. This event dramatically turned attention to the Soviet nuclear threat to the United States and, consequently, turned it away from the more remote threat of local war. It generated a climate in which increases in the American defense budget were possible, but the increases were to be for counteracting the impending Soviet ICBM capability, which threatened the United States with destruction. *Sputnik* provided the emotional impetus for a fresh appraisal of the direct defense of the United States, and the Gaither Committee provided the intellectual support.

The Gaither Committee was appointed by President Eisenhower early in 1957 to consider a proposal for an extensive fallout-shelter program in the United States. The committee was comprised of private citizens, many of whom had served under President Truman and were later to serve during the Kennedy and Johnson administrations. They included William C. Foster, who was to become director of the Arms Control and Disarmament Agency, and Jerome Wiesner, who later served as science adviser to President Kennedy. This group, like the committee that drew up NSC 68, was bound neither by current strategy nor by a budget ceiling. In its report, presented to the President and the National Security Council shortly after the launching of *Sputnik,* the committee warned for the first time of the danger of a "missile gap." It stated that unless the United States stepped up its program of intercontinental strategic force, the Soviet Union would have a larger strategic force and, moreover, would have the capability in a first strike of destroying the entire American strategic capability. The committee thus urged a substantial increase in the defense budget aimed primarily at improving the American strategic posture. The report of the committee, which has never been formally released, made recommendations similar to those of an unclassified study that was part of the Rockefeller Brothers Fund report on the United States at midcentury. These recommendations, coupled with the impact of *Sputnik,* led to a slight increase in the defense budget; the shift to a greater emphasis on local defense forces was never realized. Perhaps most important, the Gaither episode demonstrated the inability of any group, either in opposition to the President or comprised mainly of private citizens (or, as in this case, both), to influence military strategy. However, the committee — largely because many of its findings were leaked to the press — did provoke the missile-gap debate.

The reports of both the Gaither Committee and the Rockefeller Brothers Fund were influenced by a revolution in strategic analysis in the United States. The assumption of previous thinking had been that the strategic balance was in some way inherently stable. Prevailing had been an image of the nuclear powers as scorpions in a bottle who could sting each other to death but only at the price of being stung to death in return. Most of the intellectual basis for revising this image was taken from the work of Albert Wohlstetter, of the RAND Corporation. The most systematic public statement of the position was made by Wohlstetter in an article entitled "The Delicate Balance of Terror," in the January 1959 issue of *Foreign Affairs.* Wohlstetter said that by attacking its enemy's strategic forces, a country could disarm the other "scorpion" and not be stung back. This position stressed the importance of second-strike forces — that is, forces that could survive a first strike and could retaliate.

It maintained that a country should assess the vulnerability of its forces to a counterforce first strike and then should develop well-protected second-strike forces, using such techniques as hardening, dispersal, and airborne or ground alert. This view, which has not been generally accepted within the defense community, implied that there was no inherent stable balance, but rather that a country had to spend a good deal of money — including resources for research, development, communications, and control systems — to build up a credible deterrent against a determined opponent with an efficient first-strike capability. In suggesting that even for the long run a significant portion of American spending would have to be on strategic forces, this position had important implications for the allocation of defense resources.

1960 Election

Defense issues played an important part in the 1960 presidential campaign between John F. Kennedy and Richard M. Nixon. Nixon, while feeling obliged to defend the Eisenhower administration, did suggest that larger spending would be necessary. Kennedy launched a full-scale attack on the administration's defense posture, criticizing its efforts both in strategy and in the field of conventional forces. He warned of the danger of a missile gap, which would permit the Soviets to have a larger strategic force — perhaps capable of destroying the American force in a coordinated first strike — than the United States. Although this charge was clearly made in good faith, there apparently was never any real danger of a missile gap or a deterrence gap. Kennedy also suggested — accurately — that the United States had seriously neglected conventional forces and an airlift and sealift capability for them. He expressed the need for having the option to fight without the use of nuclear weapons.

The McNamara Pentagon

The election of Kennedy, his appointment of Robert S. McNamara as Secretary of Defense, and McNamara's recruitment of civilians who had worked on strategic questions for a number of years led to changes in procedures and substance.

Perhaps the most important change was in the structure of the Pentagon and in the decision-making processes. McNamara relied more on his civilian advisers than on the armed services and employed the techniques of systems analysis and cost-effectiveness analysis. The administration also introduced program budgeting—that is, organizing the budget around functions. For example, budget headings such as Strategic Offensive and Defensive Forces and General Purpose (local war) Forces were used instead of such administrative headings as Personnel, Maintenance, and Construction. This meant that spending for *Polaris* submarines would be compared with spending for Air Force *Minuteman* missiles rather than for destroyers. It also meant that the President and later Congress and the public could better understand how the defense budget was spent. In addition to the procedural changes, there were important alterations in the areas of conventional forces, general-war doctrine, and counterinsurgency.

Shortly after McNamara took over the Pentagon, programs increasing the size of the Army from twelve to sixteen combat divisions and stressing procurement, research, and development for conventional capability were initiated. This was the first noteworthy effort in this direction since World War II. Increases in the capability and readiness of the services for conventional war were increased substantially during the early 1960's in the belief that the United States should prepare for 2½ wars. Thus when President Johnson decided to send large numbers of United States troops to South Vietnam, the forces were available and equipped with nonnuclear weapons. The United States also began to urge its NATO allies to engage in a conventional buildup, and it pressed for a revision of NATO strategy to take account of the possibility of conventional wars. In 1967, despite the withdrawal of France from the unified NATO defense structure, NATO strategy was reversed in accordance with the flexible response strategy to provide a capability for conventional as well as nuclear operations. However, the other NATO countries resisted American pressure to increase the size of their ground forces.

Although the United States did develop an improved capability to fight conventionally, its action and communication policies on the relative role of conventional and nuclear forces continued to be ambiguous. It was evident, though, that the focus of official statements was shifting toward a greater emphasis on conventional forces. By the end of the Johnson administration the United States attitude toward the use of nuclear weapons in local wars had moved substantially from the assumption of the Eisenhower administration that such weapons would be used to reluctance to even contemplate using them.

Kennedy's campaign statements indicate that he expected to come into office confronted with Soviet superiority in strategic weapons. Instead, he found that the United States possessed an overwhelming strategic advantage. The administration asserted the political value of this superiority: it gave the United States greater freedom of political maneuver on international questions. At the same time, an increase in American strategic forces, with well-protected, accurate strategic systems and good command and control, was ordered. During its first year the Kennedy administration established strategic offensive force levels that were to remain constant through the 1960's. The United States built up a force of a thousand *Minuteman* missiles, fifty-four *Titans,* and forty-one *Polaris* submarines. However, the rationale for the force changed. In the early 1960's Secretary McNamara talked of the value of a "damage limiting" program to save American lives in the event of nuclear war, and the administration recommended a nationwide fallout-shelter program. By the mid-1960's, McNamara began to assert that, given the increasing Soviet nuclear capability, damage limiting was not feasible. He asserted that *assured destruction* — the maintenance of a capability to destroy an enemy after he had launched a full-scale attack — should be the sole criterion for designing United States strategic forces. In September 1967 McNamara announced two major additions to the American strategic arsenal. In a speech in San Francisco he stated that the United States had reached the "marginal" decision that it would be "prudent" to deploy a small ABM system designed to deal with the emerging Chinese nuclear threat. A week later he reported that the United States was planning to deploy MIRVs on its land-based and sea-based missiles. At the same time he stressed the increasing interaction of American and Soviet strategic forces and argued that neither country could effectively defend itself with an ABM system because the other country would respond to protect its own deterrent. He expressed the hope that talks between the United States and the Soviet Union would bring an end to what he called the "mad momentum of the arms race."

The question of how to deal with insurgency supported from the outside by Communist nations generated considerable controversy from the start of the Kennedy administration. President Kennedy came into office determined to improve American capability for counterinsurgency operations. At his urging the Army Green Berets were increased in number, and training for counterinsurgency was greatly intensified. Administration officials emphasized their belief that the most significant threats to security in the 1960's were likely to come from insurgency. In this setting and because of the growing success of Viet Cong insurgents in South Vietnam President Kennedy directed an increased American involvement in advising South Vietnam's government. In 1965 President Johnson began to approve a series of recommendations from his advisers for substantial American intervention in South Vietnam.

By 1968 opposition to American involvement in Vietnam and growing concern about the relative priorities of domestic problems and defense generated a major public debate on defense issues. The United States began the slow process of withdrawal from South Vietnam after President Johnson's March 1968 speech, in which he announced that he was ordering a partial halt to the bombing of North Vietnam and that he would not seek reelection. In 1969 the defense budget was reduced by several billion dollars in response to congressional pressure for spending cuts, and the Senate conducted a debate on the desirability of proceeding with the *Sentinel* ABM system directed against China. A decade that had begun with strong congressional and public pressure to improve American defense capabilities ended with increasing public debate about the need to reduce defense expenditures and to curtail American economic, military, and humanitarian involvement in the world.

The Nixon Doctrine and Sufficiency

President Richard Nixon directed an overall review of defense policy and decision procedures at the outset of his administration in 1969. From this review there emerged new decision procedures, a new basis for determining the appropriate size of General Purpose Forces, and some new approaches to strategic-force issues.

The new organizational arrangements were part of a revitalized National Security Council structure. Major defense issues are discussed in a Defense Program Review Committee under the chairmanship of the President's assistant for national security and including representatives of the Council of Economic Advisers, the Budget Bureau, and the Treasury as well as State, Defense, and the CIA. This committee examines not only the strategic and political implications of weapon programs but also considers financial implications in relation to domestic priorities.

An initial overall review of General Purpose Forces dealt with the question of the basis for determining how large American forces should be and how many contingencies they should prepare for. In line with the Nixon Doctrine, first announced by the President at Guam in 1969, the administration concluded that American forces should not be maintained for the purpose of dealing with subversion or guerrilla warfare. Rather, insurgency should be preempted by social and economic programs or dealt with by the policy and military forces of local governments. Even against conventional threats, the United States would primarily rely on local forces. The National Security Council considered five alternative strategies for General Purpose Forces and rejected two of them because, according to President Nixon's first report to Congress on foreign policy, they were not considered essential to United States security and would have thwarted vital domestic programs. The President's 1970 state of the world report, the first of its kind, described the foreign and defense policies of the United States and reported on the strategy selected: "In an effort to harmonize doctrine and capability, we chose what is best described as the '½ war' strategy. Under it we will maintain in peacetime General Purpose Forces adequate for simultaneously meeting a major Communist attack in either Europe or Asia, assisting allies against non-Chinese threats in Asia, and contending with a contingency elsewhere."

In part this strategy was justified on the grounds that America's nuclear capability would effectively deter large-scale aggression. However, the Nixon administration continued to be ambiguous about when the United States would use nuclear weapons and maintained the policy of equipping and training forces for conventional warfare. After the initial NSC review of General Purpose Forces, questions remained about the capability needed to meet the new strategy and how substantially General Purpose Forces would decline as American forces were withdrawn from South Vietnam.

The Nixon administration also conducted an intensive review of strategic forces. During the 1968 presidential election campaign Nixon had argued for the need to reestablish American nuclear superiority. However, as a result of an NSC review of strategic issues, the administration concluded that, given Soviet nuclear power and its ability to respond to improvements in American strategic forces, superiority was impossible to maintain. The administration then ruled out any substantial increase in American strategic forces, and it rejected arguments for cutting back on planned programs on the grounds that such cuts might encourage the Soviet Union to seek nuclear superiority. Adopting the label of "nuclear sufficiency," the administration warned that, if the Soviet buildup in strategic forces that began in 1965 continued, the United States would consider expanding its own programs. The President's state of the world report also stated that further review would focus on the question of how *assured destruction* should be defined and whether it should be the only measure for designing strategic forces.

Even before its overall review was completed, the administration faced the question of how to deal with the growing congressional and public opposition to the *Sentinel* ABM program. In announcing a revised *Safeguard* ABM program, President Nixon committed his administration to avoiding programs that would seem to threaten the Soviet deterrent. He directed that the ABM deployment be redesigned to reduce the possibility of its growing into a major system deployed against a Soviet attack. While maintaining an interest in defense against China, Nixon emphasized defense of the United States *Minuteman* force against a growing Soviet offensive capability. After intensive debate during the summer of 1969, the Senate approved the *Safeguard* program when a 50–50 vote defeated an amendment to eliminate the deployment. In 1970 the Senate again approved a deployment but only after its Armed Services Committee had removed those parts of the administration plan designed to begin an area defense of the United States and limiting the program to defense of *Minuteman* missile sites.

The review of the American strategic program proceeded along with preparations for Strategic Arms Limitation Talks (SALT) with the Soviet Union. These talks, which began in late 1969, were the first serious effort of the two nuclear superpowers to end the nuclear arms race.

CHAPTER FIVE

SOVIET MILITARY STRATEGY

Throughout the postwar period the United States has viewed the Soviet Union as its chief military opponent. The main thrust of American policy has been toward the deterrence of military actions by the Soviet Union or its allies. In the 1960's attention focused on China as a separate potential military opponent. This chapter is a discussion of Soviet military doctrine, particularly as it relates to Soviet strategy in dealing with the American strategic nuclear threat and with Europe.

Before turning to the substance of Soviet military doctrine, we will consider briefly the nature of our sources of information about Soviet and Chinese military doctrine. Statements issued by the two governments are one source. The amount of literature from the Soviet Union is much greater than that from China, but both countries release statements of general foreign policy and, in the case of the Soviet Union, statements on military issues. The Soviets have released some books dealing specifically with military strategy, the most important of these was *Military Strategy,* edited by Soviet General Sokolovsky. This book, which purports to be a comprehensive statement of Soviet doctrine, has been widely analyzed in the West as a source of insight into Soviet military strategy. Much material on Sino-Soviet military relations and the military strategy of the two countries has been revealed in the polemics of the Sino-Soviet dispute.

A second major source of data — one perhaps too little exploited — is the actions of the two countries. We should be able to learn much more about Sino-Soviet military doctrine from actions in Korea, Berlin, and Cuba than from articles in military journals.

Finally, the military-budget decisions and deployment decisions of the two countries can be examined. Both countries publish a single one-line item on defense in their annual budget but obviously spend a good deal more on defense. Much work has been done on the size and form of the Soviet defense budgets, some of it released by the Joint Economic Committee of Congress. Other material on the output of the two countries' defense budgets is available in an Institute for Strategic Studies annual pamphlet, *Military Balance;* in the American defense-budget hearings; and in such American publications as *Aviation Week*. Studies published by RAND Corporation are also available; authors of such studies have access to classified data.

In seeking to understand Soviet military doctrine, we need to keep in mind that the Soviet government, party, and bureaucracy do not have a single view of defense matters. Budget and deployment decisions are as much influenced by organizational constraints and by bureaucratic maneuvering and domestic political considerations as by doctrinal considerations.

Though our understanding of Soviet and Chinese military doctrine is more limited than our understanding of American doctrine, we do have a working knowledge of Soviet policy, at least for the early years of the postwar period. We can even say a great deal with some confidence about current Soviet doctrine.

Soviet General-War Strategy

The primary concern of the Soviet Union's military policy during the entire postwar period has been the deterrence of an American nuclear attack. In the period until the mid-1950's, the Soviet Union was completely dependent for deterrence of an American attack on threats to retaliate against American allies rather than against the United States, because the Soviets had no significant capability to attack the American homeland. During this early period the major Soviet military deterrent was a large ground force capable of seizing and holding Western Europe. In addition to its large ground army, the Soviet Union placed great emphasis on air defense. The Soviets have continued up to the present time to spend a much greater percentage of their defense budget on active defense than the United States does. In the early 1960's the Soviet Union began to deploy a large air defense system known in the West as the Tallinn system. The system, which the Soviets were continuing to expand in 1970, was apparently designed against the B-70 bomber, which the United States considered deploying in the early 1960's. In the early stages of its deployment, some American intelligence analysts believed that Tallinn might be an ABM system. However, by 1970 there was agreement that this was not the case and that the only Soviet ABM was a small system centered around Moscow. The size and shape of the Soviet defensive forces seem to have been guided and influenced by bureaucratic tendencies as much as, or perhaps more than, by a positive strategic doctrine. The doctrine, insofar as it existed, apparently aimed at using active defense and passive civil defense in order to reduce the damage that the United States could do to the Soviet Union.

At the same time, immediately following World War II, the Soviet Union engaged in a crash program for the development of atomic weapons. The existence of the program demonstrates the danger of relying on writings from the Soviet Union, which, until after the death of Stalin, claimed no interest in atomic warfare. Rather, it was suggested that Stalin believed that "permanent operating factors" emphasizing the social and economic structure of the countries would determine the outcome of a war. In fact, decision-makers in the Soviet Union recognized the great importance of atomic weapons and the effect they would have on warfare and on diplomacy. In the postwar period the Soviet Union developed atomic weapons quickly and hydrogen bombs even more quickly, perhaps even before the United States. At the same time the Soviets launched a crash research and development program on delivery systems, including long-range bombers and intercontinental ballistic missiles.

The final part of the Soviet plan for deterrence was the adoption of a relatively moderate foreign policy designed to deter politically American overreaction. The Soviet leaders recognized that they were in a state of military weakness and, consequently, could not afford to press too far in attempting to expand the area under Communist control.

Soviet Intercontinental Capability. In the middle 1950's the Soviet Union began to develop some capability for attacking the United States with a small strategic bomber force. However, its strategic nuclear force was still substantially limited. The Soviet Union decided not to produce nearly as many strategic delivery vehicles — bombers in the 1950's and ICBMs in the late 1950's and early 1960's — as it could have. Thus in 1965 the Soviet Union remained substantially inferior to the United States in quantity and quality of strategic forces. The Soviets had tested a 100-megaton nuclear warhead and had built some large ICBMs capable of carrying multimegaton weapons, but their total ICBM force was only several hundred, compared to the American force of 1,054 ICBMs. Soviet submarine firing missiles were primitive — each submarine carried only a few missiles and had to surface to fire. However, the Soviet leadership had decided a few years earlier to change this situation, and signs of a new posture began to emerge.

In 1970 the Soviet Union passed the United States in numbers of deployed ICBMs. The Soviet force then consisted of several types of missile. Most plentiful was a missile called in the West the SS-11, which was liquid fueled but otherwise closely resembled the *Minuteman.* The part of the force that created the most concern in the United States was the so-called SS-9, a large missile capable of carrying a substantial payload. Concern had increased in 1969 when the Soviets began testing a Multiple Re-entry Vehicle of three warheads, which some American analysts feared could be targeted to destroy the *Minuteman* force. In the late 1960's the Soviets had begun to deploy a submarine that closely resembled the United States submarines that carry *Polaris* missiles. Each vessel of this so-called Y class had sixteen missile tubes, was nuclear powered, and could fire from under water.

The Soviet leaders clearly had determined to remove any impression of inferiority in strategic forces. When they would level off their buildup was far from certain in 1970.

Current Strategic Doctrine. Soviet statements and actions suggest that Soviet thinking about strategic questions closely parallels Western thought. The Soviets accept the critical importance of surprise and of the first strike in the early hours of a general nuclear war. They acknowledge also that the early stages of a war can be decisive, although they continue to discuss the phase of large-scale ground fighting that follows a strategic exchange (and seem to assume that they could invade and capture Western Europe). The most important items in their budget and in their policy statements relate to warfare in the early hours and the strategic nuclear exchange.

The Soviets are aware of the importance of developing strategic forces that are relatively invulnerable to a first strike. Their second-generation missiles appear to be smaller and better protected than the first-generation missiles; the Soviets are also building up a submarine-launched missile capability that is relatively invulnerable. They have always put great stress on the importance of command and control — for internal political reasons, tied up with their desire to ensure that the Soviet Army could never successfully challenge the Communist Party, as well as for strategic reasons.

In late 1957 the Soviets began to talk about the great destruction that would result on both sides from a general nuclear war. Premier Khrushchev publicly rejected what was identified as the Marxist-

Leninist notion of the inevitability of war and suggested instead that war could be avoided because there were reasonable men on both sides and that war had to be avoided because of the great destruction it would bring. The Soviets stressed the deterrence that would result from their threat to destroy cities with multimegaton weapons. In their polemics with the Chinese on the question of nuclear war, they accused the Chinese of not sufficiently understanding the destructive power of nuclear weapons. They pointed out that nuclear weapons do not observe class distinctions.

In 1969 the Soviet Union and the United States began Strategic Arms Limitation Talks, at which negotiators for the two countries engaged for the first time in serious discussions of strategic doctrine. During the preliminary round of talks in Helsinki, Finland, the Soviet delegate indicated that the Soviets shared the basic American position that deterrence was based on the ability of each side to inflict massive damage on the other after receiving a first strike. The Soviets agreed that if one side sought to take away the other's deterrent by substantially increasing its offensive or defensive capability the other side would respond to offset the advantage. Both at the conference and in public statements Soviet leaders implied that the Soviet goal was nuclear parity and not superiority, but they also warned that they would not permit the United States to regain the superiority it had in the 1960's.

The Soviets are undoubtedly concerned that the American MIRV and ABM programs would reestablish American superiority and would require them to invest additional large sums in devising new strategic capabilities. For this reason the Soviet leadership may consider its alternatives to be an agreed-to end to further escalation of the arms race and massive additional expenditures.

Soviet Strategy for Europe

One key element of Soviet strategy for Europe has already been mentioned — the notion that Western Europe can be used to deter the United States from attacking the Soviet Union.

The most blatant use of Soviet military power in the postwar period has occurred in Eastern Europe. In the early postwar period the Soviet Army seized control in this area and put into power Communist governments that were then totally subservient to Moscow. The continued presence of the Soviet Army in Central Europe has discouraged countries from leaving the Soviet bloc, and, of course, the forces were actually used in East Germany, Hungary, and Czechoslovakia.

The Soviet Union apparently never even contemplated the overt use of military force against Western Europe. Evidence now suggests that the Soviet Union did not consider a march to the English Channel, the threat upon which NATO has concentrated. The Soviet fear of atomic retaliation by the United States was always present, as well as recognition of the problems that would ensue in trying to bring Western Europe under Communist control. Finally, the Soviets have probably been aware of the unreliability of the East European armies and populations and hence the vulnerability of their supply lines. However, even if the Soviets never contemplated a march to the channel, the relative military balance in Central Europe has influenced the political evolution of countries on both sides of the iron curtain.

The Soviet posture toward Western Europe has been, and continues to be, a defensive and deterrent one. The positioning of Soviet ground forces in Eastern Europe and the limited logistical capability of these forces suggests an orientation primarily toward defense against a Western attack. Perhaps for this reason the Soviet Army has produced in quantity fighters and surface-to-air missiles. The size of the Soviet Army in Europe has been a matter of some confusion in Western analyses. In the early postwar period the Soviets were credited with 175 divisions, a number that remained constant despite reorganizations of the Soviet Army and reductions in the number of ground troops. Recent estimates by the United States have been less than half that number, and it appears that the Soviet Union does not have now, and may never have had, overwhelming conventional superiority on the central front in Europe.

Apparently the Soviets have been no more successful than the West in developing a coherent doctrine for the employment of tactical nuclear weapons. Soviet forces are capable of fighting both conventionally and with tactical nuclear weapons; however, the Soviet tactical nuclear arsenal is much smaller and much less sophisticated than that of the United States. Not until the mid-1960's did the Soviets begin to introduce somewhat smaller tactical nuclear weapons into the operating arsenals of their ground troops. The Soviets seem to believe that if nuclear weapons were used, it would be over a large area and with relatively large warheads.

The major Soviet use of military force in Western Europe has been as a threat in order to accomplish specific political purposes. Much of this effort has centered on Berlin. The Soviets have attempted to use their conventional superiority in the local area to force the West out of the city or at least into accepting East German sovereignty over the access routes to Berlin. They have warned nations that have permitted American nuclear weapons to be stationed in their territory that they have left themselves open to the danger of Soviet nuclear attack. The most specific Soviet threats ensued in 1960, when the Soviets shot down an American U-2 reconnaissance plane over Soviet territory. The Soviets warned that they would destroy with a missile any base from which an American U-2 flying over the Soviet Union had taken off or landed.

The basic Soviet aims in Europe have been to consolidate control over Eastern Europe, to gain control over, or at least neutralize, Germany, and to drive the United States from Europe. A combination of military pressure and various political tactics including peace offensives have been used in order to accomplish these objectives. The importance of these goals has varied through the postwar period, but, in all cases, the Soviet military power has served as an important backdrop.

China

The Soviet Union signed a treaty of alliance with China in 1950. The treaty, which neither side has repudiated, commits the Soviet

Union to aid China if attacked by Japan or a country allied to Japan. During crises in East Asia on several occasions during the 1950's, Soviet leaders affirmed their determination to assist China in the event of an American attack on the Chinese mainland. However, what action they would have taken is far from clear.

During the 1960's the Soviet military began to be concerned with the possibility of a military clash with China. In the late 1960's there was a substantial buildup of Soviet forces on the Sino-Soviet border, and there were several border clashes between the two Communist giants. In 1969 the Soviets, by warning many governments of the danger of Chinese aggression, appeared to be laying the groundwork for justifying a preemptive strike against China's nuclear installations. The Chinese accused the Soviets of preparing to attack. The crisis was eased by the agreement of the two countries to open talks to resolve the border dispute, but there is no doubt that the Soviet leaders continue to view China as a potential military opponent.

CHAPTER SIX

CHINESE MILITARY STRATEGY

With the growing belief in the unwillingness of the Soviet Union to use its military force and with the growth of Chinese military power, particularly nuclear power, the People's Republic of China has received increasing attention from military strategists and defense planners. One manifestation of this development, accelerated by the Sino-Soviet split and the war in Vietnam, is the consideration given by the United States to the installation of a ballistic-missile defense directed against China. However, much less has been written about China than about the Soviet Union. This chapter is an examination of Chinese military strategy in the context of Chinese foreign policy.

The events of the Cultural Revolution have made it clear that the leaders of the Chinese government have had the same types of disputes about strategic and budgetary issues as other governments have. The professional military leaders have pressed for higher defense budgets, military cooperation with the Soviet Union, and autonomy for the People's Liberation Army. Mao has sought to use the army as an instrument of revolution within China and to employ it for political and psychological advantage. Those in the government charged with economic planning have sought to channel funds away from the military to economic development. Nevertheless, one can discern broad lines of agreed-upon Chinese doctrine.

Chinese foreign policy objectives have been, and continue to be, subordinated to domestic objectives: the preservation of the regime, the continuation of the revolution, and the economic growth and industrialization of society. Defense budgets have been modest, certainly in contrast to the generally held image of a militant and militarist China, and even by universal standards of expenditures on defense. The defense spending appears to be primarily for defending Chinese territory against a Nationalist Chinese invasion or perhaps an American invasion, rather than for offensive operations that would require, for example, strong airpower.

In addition, the Chinese have concentrated on avoiding a clash with the United States. Chinese Communist strategy during the Chinese civil war was influenced by the necessity to forestall United States entry into the war and to end the war without provoking an American attack. Despite the great importance the Chinese have attached to capturing Taiwan and eliminating the regime there, they have not engaged in any activities that could have brought them into a direct military clash with the United States. Since June 1950, when the United States committed itself to the defense of Taiwan, there has not been any Chinese attempt to take Taiwan. The only actions have been against the offshore islands of Quemoy and Matsu, and these attacks have been cautiously maneuvered. In Indochina and India as well, whatever the Chinese motivations may have been, the restraint of their actions has been due in part to fear of provoking an American attack.

Turning more specifically to foreign policy objectives of the Peking regime, we can identify some that are peculiarly "Chinese." The urgency involved in their attainment, or the way in which Peking seeks to attain them, clearly is influenced by the fact that the Peking regime is a Communist regime, but these objectives are ones that any strong Chinese government would have. There are other objectives that a non-Communist Chinese government would not have and that are equally important to Chinese policy.

The most important national interest objective is the recovery of territories that are part of China or that the country's leaders consider part of China and, consequently, try to regain for the regime. The major action for this objective has been the conquest of Tibet (which the Chinese Nationalists supported). The current outstanding irredenta is, or course, Taiwan, and gaining control of this territory has been a primary foreign policy objective since 1949.

Closely related to the incorporation of Taiwan into the Peking regime is the elimination of the rival regime on Taiwan, which claims to be the government of all China. The Chinese have adopted a policy of not recognizing or entering into diplomatic relations with any country that has relations with the Taiwan regime.

Finally, the establishment of Chinese dominance in Asia is an important objective, although it receives less attention than the others mentioned so far. It is one that would be pursued by any strong government in control of the mainland of China.

Other interests derive from the Communist ideology of Chinese leaders. The Peking regime wishes to increase the area under Communist control, as distinguished from the area under Chinese control. This has led in part to a willingness to support Communist regimes — in particular, Communist regimes that, according to the Chinese, take the correct Marxist-Leninist line. Albania is a good example. The Chinese have been giving this country both substantial foreign aid, given Chinese capability, and vigorous diplomatic support. The Chinese now attach great importance to having the Communist parties pursue what the Chinese consider to be the correct line rather than a modern-revisionist line, notably in determining the best way to expand the area under Communist control and to bring about the overthrow of imperialism and then of capitalist and non-Communist regimes. It is difficult to maintain that the Chinese did not give, for their own sake, high priority to the establishment of Communist regimes in Africa, Latin America, and the Middle East. The Chinese cannot really hope to make major gains in terms of purely Chinese interest from the establishment of Communist regimes in these areas, yet evidence from the Sino-Soviet dispute suggests that they are willing to have the international Communist movement pursue the "correct" line at the expense of deterioration of their relations with the Soviets.

The Role of Force

Turning more specifically to strategic issues, we may ask: How do the Chinese feel force can, and should, be used? Mao has said that power comes from the barrel of a gun and that politics should control the gun. For the Peking regime, force is a legitimate instrument of both internal and external policy; it must be put at all times under political control and must be used in limited, controlled ways in the pursuit of particular foreign policy objectives. The Chinese see nothing wrong with using force for political purposes, and they have demonstrated their willingness to use force for a variety of specific objectives.

The fundamental principle of Maoist military doctrine is the notion of going from a weak position to a strong position in which a country's objectives can be realized. Maoism holds that with a very small force a country can triumph ultimately against overwhelming odds by gradually increasing its strength while diminishing the strength of its opponent. The Chinese used this strategy in the civil war and are now trying to follow it in their foreign policy.

The statement that a country should strategically despise its enemy but tactically respect him — a doctrine the Chinese specifically apply to the United States — simply means that in the long run a country can defeat its enemy by using the proper tactics but in the short run must recognize that the enemy is stronger and, therefore, must be respected. It is in this light that we should examine such statements as "The United States is a paper tiger." It means that in the long run the United States can be defeated by proper strategy; it does not mean that nuclear weapons cannot destroy China, if the United States chooses to use them now. We must view the statement that man will triumph over weapons similarly. It does not mean that if a nuclear weapon and a man are in the same place, the nuclear weapon cannot explode and kill the man; it means that in the long run what will determine the political orientation of countries is the views of men and not the nature of the weapon system. This was true in China; this, the Chinese believe, is true in Indochina; and they believe ultimately that it will be true everywhere. Communism can spread by gaining the allegiance of men regardless of who controls what weapons in the short run.

Nuclear War

There is a widespread view that the Chinese do not understand nuclear war, do not fear nuclear war, and, in fact, even desire nuclear war, and that they lack an understanding of the realities of the nuclear age. This completely false view has been spread largely by the Soviet Union, because it happens to fulfill a Soviet objective: to convince the West that the Soviet Union wants a détente because it has Chinese lunatics on its border. However, if one looks at what the Chinese say and what they have done in various crisis situations, their point of view becomes clear: nuclear war would, in fact, be a great disaster for the world and, in particular, for China and the Communist regime. They are under no illusion that the leaders of China, as well as the industrialization of China that the leaders have directed, would be spared, in even a rather small nuclear war.

They probably believe that communism, not capitalism, would survive as the world system of government and that China would survive as a political entity. In addition, the Chinese have contended, especially with the Soviets, that to emphasize the destructiveness of nuclear war and to make speeches about how many people would be killed in how many minutes in a nuclear war is politically self-defeating. It exposes a country to political blackmail by its opponent with nuclear weapons; it demoralizes a country and is exceptionally dangerous when that country does not have nuclear weapons. It is unreasonable to expect the Chinese to stress the dangers of nuclear war when they have only a small number of nuclear weapons and are facing two potential opponents with massive nuclear strength. The Chinese have sought to capitalize on the misconception that they do not fear nuclear war. In the early 1960's they were tending in this direction, and the standard line of

Western analysts was to say that while the Chinese assert that they do not fear nuclear war, they really do. Nor is it clear that the Chinese are not asserting that nuclear war would be good for China. This is partly a recognition on their part that to play the role of lunatic can be in some situations a source of strength, if their opponents are convinced that the Chinese are not afraid of their opponents' weapons. However, it can also be a source of weakness in the sense that China's enemies might be more intent on trying to destroy the Peking regime if they thought that the Chinese were lunatics.

There has been, we are told, a major revision in the Soviet outlook on war; the Soviets no longer believe that nuclear war is inevitable. This is not so great a change as it is sometimes made out to be; but, whatever kind of revision it is, the Chinese have also accepted it. The Chinese believe that war is inevitable — wars of national revolution or wars between capitalist societies — but that nuclear war between the Communist bloc and the capitalist bloc is not inevitable.

Closely related to Chinese concepts of nuclear war is the Chinese image of the role of the strategic balance in international politics. From the image often held — that to the Chinese, men are more important than weapons and that nuclear weapons do not really count — it might be surmised that the Chinese attach little importance to the strategic balance; in fact, the reverse is true. The Chinese have placed more emphasis on the nuclear balance than either the United States or the Soviet Union. They have attempted to some extent to measure historical periods by the nature of the nuclear balance. The famous Chinese assertion in 1957 that the East Wind was prevailing over the West Wind is a reflection of the importance the Chinese attach to the nuclear balance and their belief that historical periods and historical possibilities change when the nuclear balance changes. The Chinese believed that a major change would occur in 1957 for two reasons: they thought the Soviets were beoming stronger than the Americans and that the Soviet Union was about to give them their own nuclear capability. By 1960 they realized that neither of these two predictions would, in fact, materialize. This realization, plus China's increasing isolation from the Soviet Union, has resulted in a much more vigorous pursuit of an independent Chinese nuclear capability.

The fundamental Chinese motivation for acquiring a nuclear capability is based on the following reasoning: all great powers have nuclear weapons; China is a great power; therefore, China must have nuclear weapons. The Chinese desire for nuclear weapons goes back to 1946, when the Chinese saw that atomic weapons would be an important component of power and decided that in the long run China would have to become an atomic power. The desire for nuclear weapons is a basic drive of the regime — one that is unlikely to be affected by the details of technology or the cost involved.

A second, more concrete objective for having nuclear weapons is to deter an American or Soviet attack on China. It is not yet clear what kind of nuclear delivery capability the Chinese will develop as a deterrent. In 1970 the Chinese capability continued to be limited to airplanes with a limited range. Although the Chinese have been working on Medium-Range Ballistic Missiles for some time — and the American government has been predicting their imminent deployment since 1965 — the Chinese do not yet have any operational MRBMs. They are working on ICBMs but American government estimates are that they will not have a significant capability until the 1980's.

Nuclear weapons are important to the Chinese as a means of increasing their power within the Communist world. The Chinese feel that if they are ever going to challenge successfully the regime in Moscow, they will have to do it on a basis of increased power — namely, nuclear power. Finally, they see nuclear weapons as being of marginal value in support of their political objectives in Asia — as a threat against Asian countries.

Conventional War

When we examine the role of conventional forces as an instrument of Chinese foreign policy, we see most strikingly that the Chinese have a strong desire to avoid major conventional war, primarily for two reasons: the economic cost involved in preparing for a major conventional war — the amount of equipment and training that would be necessary — and the economic cost of participating in the war in terms of resources used and possible destruction. In addition, probably as important, is the realization that any large-scale deployment of conventional forces runs the danger of provoking an American attack. The Chinese have been willing to use limited kinds of military force for specific purposes in the Taiwan Straits and on the Sino-Indian border.

The Chinese have used major force in only two kinds of situations: first, when they felt there was no danger of intervention by an outside power, for example, in Tibet, where they thought that the territory they were attacking was part of China and consequently committed what is the clearest case of overt aggression in the postwar period; secondly, when they felt the alternative of not using major military force was more dangerous than engaging in this kind of encounter, as in Korea.

In conclusion, what can be said about the Chinese long-run view of their own, and the world, situation? Most important to them is the establishment of China as a major world, and nuclear, power. Peking also envisions the establishment of Chinese hegemony in Asia, the elimination of American bases there, and recognition by all Asian countries of China's dominance. Further, they see the destruction of the Republic of China and the incorporation of Taiwan into the Peking regime, although they have no clear notion of how this is going to come about. They view the United States and the Soviet Union as their principal enemies. As long as Mao is alive, improved relations with either country is unlikely. The post-Mao leadership may be split over the question of whether to seek a fundamental improvement in relations with either Moscow or Washington.

In terms of relations with other countries — Japan, Western Europe, the underdeveloped areas — Chinese views are probably not clearly defined. They fear the growing power of Japan; that they can establish friendly relations with West European countries, in order to make credit and trade agreements; and that in Africa and Latin America the number of revolutionary regimes will increase. They probably are not optimistic about any of these occurring — to the extent that they want them to — in the next ten or fifteen years.

CHAPTER SEVEN

GENERAL WAR: THE STRATEGY OF SUFFICIENCY

President Nixon, early in his administration, characterized the nuclear policy he would pursue as "sufficiency." Statements by administration officials indicated that four criteria would determine the "sufficiency" of American strategic forces:

1. *Assured destruction:* The United States would at all times have the capability to respond with high confidence to a Soviet surprise attack on the United States homeland and to destroy a substantial part of Soviet society.
2. *Crisis stability:* Strategic forces of the United States would be designed not to create instability during a crisis whereby one or both sides would be tempted to launch a preemptive nuclear attack.
3. *Relative advantage:* The United States would seek to avoid a situation in which the Soviet Union might be able to gain a substantial advantage in terms of relative destruction in a nuclear war.
4. *Damage denial:* The United States would develop a capability for denying other powers, including China, the ability to inflict damage on the United States with their strategic nuclear forces.

The President and other administration officials indicated that the United States would design its strategic forces so they would not appear to be threatening the Soviet Union's assured deterrence capability. The United States would not build a large-area ABM system nor develop a capability to target hard Soviet missiles, for either of these developments could appear to threaten the Soviet deterrent and force the Soviets to increase the size of their own strategic force.

This chapter is an examination of the criteria for sufficiency set forth by the Nixon administration and of two weapon decisions.

Assured Destruction

During the last years of the Johnson administration the strategic doctrine of the United States appeared more and more to focus on assured destruction. As originally defined by Secretary of Defense Robert McNamara, assured destruction meant that the United States would develop a capability to destroy 25 per cent of the Soviet population and a similar percentage of Soviet industry after the Soviet Union had executed a successful surprise nuclear attack against the United States. McNamara thought that the ability to inflict this damage with high confidence would be a strong deterrent against a Soviet nuclear attack. When McNamara first defined assured destruction, the United States had a substantially larger capability than the Soviet Union, and he argued that no additions to the American strategic force were necessary. In establishing criteria for assured destruction, the Pentagon advanced the notion of a greater than expected Soviet threat — that is, a threat larger than that postulated by the intelligence community. The assured destruction capability of the United States provided leeway so that even if the Soviets developed a greater than expected threat, the United States would still be able to maintain high confidence in its ability to inflict 25 per cent fatalities on the Soviet Union. The Pentagon's calculations took into account only prompt fatalities from blast and local radiation and not fatalities that might result from fallout over a large area, fire storms, or other secondary effects of a large nuclear attack.

There is agreement that America must be able to inflict heavy damage on the Soviet Union after the Soviets have executed a first strike and that no Soviet leadership would order a first strike if it was certain beyond any doubt that a large part of the Soviet Union would be destroyed in return. Until the end of the 1960's, calculations to determine whether the United States had sufficient forces were made on a conservative basis. However, as the Soviet strategic capability has grown, the question of whether the United States should remain confident of its assured destruction capability, given the factors used to calculate that capability, has arisen. Are the calculations relevant and sufficient?

Is it necessary for the United States to be able to destroy 25 per cent of the Soviet population or would a smaller amount of damage be sufficient? The 25 per cent figure was apparently decided on because one-fourth of the Soviet population lives in a few large cities. If one wanted to destroy more than 25 per cent of the Soviet population, many additional Soviet cities would have to be destroyed. This is a rationale for not trying to destroy *more* than 25 per cent of the Soviet population, but the question of whether a 15 per cent or even a 10 per cent destruction would not be sufficient to deter the Soviets in any conceivable situation in which deterrence was operating remains open. The United States assured destruction calculations assume that Soviet systems work about as well as the American intelligence community predicts and that United States systems work less effectively than they could. For example, it is assumed that American penetration would not work completely effectively against a Soviet ballistic-missile defense system.

Other questions about the assured destruction calculations concern the number of strategic systems that are necessary. The United States has maintained three separate strategic systems — sea-based ballistic missiles, land-based ballistic missiles, and bombers — each of which is required to have a capability to destroy 25 per cent of the Soviet population in the event of a nuclear attack. Two questions have been raised about this requirement. Must each of the three systems be able to destroy 25 per cent of the Soviet population or would destruction by a combination of any two systems, for example, be sufficient? A more fundamental question is whether the United States should maintain three separate strategic systems or whether one or two systems that could with high confidence destroy 25 per cent of the Soviet population would be sufficient.

The nature of the threat American strategists should plan for has also raised issues. The original calculations were in terms of a greater than expected threat. An alternative would be to design forces against the threat that the intelligence community considers most likely, leaving some leeway in case of a threat larger than that but one still considered possible.

Each of these considerations affects assured destruction calculations, and all together they could determine whether substantial additions to the American strategic force were needed. Modifying the assured destruction requirements could lead to the conclusion that the United States did not need to deploy MIRVs in the early 1970's, and maintaining the strict requirements established in the 1960's could justify substantial increases in American strategic forces. Now that the Soviet Union has achieved basic strategic parity with the United States, stability might be jeopardized if the United States seeks high-confidence assured destruction capability. If the Soviet Union were to seek the same kind of assured destruction capability, the situation would become unstable because both sides could not simultaneously have the same high confidence that, for example, five years in the future they would have assured destruction capability. If both established such criteria, both would constantly have to add to their strategic forces, and neither could ever be certain that in the future it would have the desired capability. Thus, there is a conflict between the desire to level off the strategic arms race and the goal of maintaining the requisites for assured destruction, which paradoxically had been created in the early 1960's to justify a leveling off of American strategic expenditures.

Perhaps the most fundamental criticism of assured destruction is that it focuses on the wrong decision-makers. Requirements for assured destruction were developed from the point of view of American policymakers concerned that the United States leaders be sure that the United States would have the ability to destroy 25 per cent of the Soviet population in the event of a Soviet first strike, Critics point out that what was necessary for deterrence was to assure the Soviet leaders that the Soviet Union would be destroyed by an American attack. This meant that American strategists had to look at the calculations from the viewpoint of the Soviet leaders and ask what was necessary and sufficient to deter them. For example, if the Soviet leadership believed that there was a 5 per cent chance of 25 per cent destruction, that might be sufficient to deter them, even though assured destruction called for 100 per cent certainty on the part of Americans that that amount of damage could be inflicted. However, there is no way to be sure what calculations the Soviet leaders would actually make in a crisis situation. Their own assessment of the strategic balance might be made on an entirely different basis from that of the Americans, and, if so, American assured destruction calculations might be totally irrelevant to a Soviet decision about whether to launch a nuclear attack. (One of the important purposes of the Strategic Arms Limitation Talks is to discover how the Soviets make strategic calculations. Because of what is learned at the talks, it may be possible to develop criteria for strategic deterrence that would reflect the approach the Soviet leaders would actually take.)

Despite these criticisms, American strategists agree that the United States needs a capability to respond with high confidence to a Soviet attack and to destroy a substantial part of the Soviet Union. What is in dispute is precisely how to calculate the capability required for this purpose and whether at any given time specific new weapon systems need to be procured to maintain an adequate deterrent.

Crisis Stability

Few critics challenge the second criterion of sufficiency — namely, that there should be no incentive for a first strike in a crisis. However, questions are raised about how one calculates crisis stability and how it interacts with other criteria. The basic assumption for crisis stability is that neither side would see an advantage in striking first if it believed a nuclear war might occur. If one side believed that the amount of damage it would suffer would be substantially larger if it struck second, it might be tempted to strike first. The other side, fearing an attack, might be tempted to strike. Thus if both sides have forces vulnerable to a first strike, reciprocal fear of surprise attack would arise and would increase the danger that during a crisis a nuclear attack would be launched. To avoid this danger neither the United States nor the Soviet Union should maintain strategic forces that could be attacked and destroyed in a crisis.

From this perspective the Nixon administration expressed concern about the ability of its land-based missiles to survive if the Soviet Union developed a force of highly accurate MIRV-armed missiles. It was argued that, even though the United States would continue to have an effective assured destruction capability in its sea-based forces, the fact that the Soviet Union could destroy a large part of the American land-based force in a first strike would lead to instability.

Critics argue that as long as the United States could destroy 25 per cent of the Soviet population in a second strike and as long as the Soviet Union could do the same to the United States, there would be no incentive to strike first to destroy a part of the other side's strategic force.

A question has been raised about how much crisis stability should affect the design of American strategic forces. Should the United States buy new strategic systems to be certain that the amount of damage it could do the Soviet Union in a second strike is essentially the same as the amount of damage it could do in a first strike? Without agreement between the two sides, it might be extremely difficult to get to a situation in which there is absolutely no incentive for either side to strike first.

Relative Advantage

The third and fourth criteria of strategic sufficiency raise more questions, with critics challenging not only the method of determining what forces are needed to meet the criteria but also whether the criteria were relevant to nuclear deterrence.

The criterion of relative advantage to the United States as a result of a nuclear war is based on the belief that the Soviet Union might be tempted to launch a nuclear attack, or at least might be able to get some political advantage from its strategic forces, if there were situations in which the United States would suffer appreciably more damage than the Soviet Union. President Nixon expressed this concern in his 1970 state of the world message. He suggested an example in which the Soviet Union would destroy all America's fixed land-based missile force and would confront the United States with the choice of doing nothing or firing its remaining forces to inflict damage on the Soviet Union only to see the Soviet Union inflict substantially more damage on the United States in return.

The search for high confidence in equal damage presents several problems. First is the question of whether the relative advantage criterion is relevant above a certain level. If the United States continues to have the capability to inflict 25 per cent fatalities, does it make any difference if the Soviets could inflict 40 per cent fatalities? Supporters of the criterion point out that assured destruction calculations are artificial; these calculations assume that the side striking first will launch all its weapons against the strategic forces of the defending nation while the defending nation will fire all its surviving missiles against the cities of the attacking country. They point out that in any conceivable situation of nuclear war the forces of both sides are likely to be used in some other way, the attacking side, for example, holding out some of its weapons to attack cities and the defending side directing some of its strategic forces against remaining missile and bomber targets. They argue that it is important to ensure in a wide range of situations that the attacking side would have no major advantage. However, the attempt to ensure no advantage in any one of a wide range of situations poses threats to crisis stability.

If the United States were to develop a capability to inflict equal damage on the Soviet Union in a range of situations, it would have to develop flexible strategic forces with extreme accuracy and reliability, which almost certainly would give it an advantage if it struck first. If the United States was sure that it would never suffer less damage than the Soviet Union, it would be almost certain to create a capability that in Soviet eyes would suggest that the United States would suffer considerably less damage if it struck first.

Some critics of relative advantage argue that it does not go far enough. They suggest that the United States seek strategic superiority — that is, the ability always to inflict considerably greater damage on the Soviet Union than the Soviet Union can inflict on the United States. These critics suggest that the Soviet Union would be tempted in a situation of parity to use strategic forces for political advantage, perhaps in Western Europe. Only if the United States has a clear superiority could it effectively defend Western Europe against nuclear attack. The response to these critics is simply that it is impossible for the United States to maintain this kind of strategic superiority in light of Soviet strategic capabilities. The Soviets will increase the size of their strategic forces to deny politically useful superiority to the United States.

Damage Denial

The fourth criterion of strategic sufficiency focuses not on the Soviet Union but rather on China and at least in theory, other potential nuclear powers. The criterion suggests that the United States should not rely simply on deterrence to prevent a Chinese nuclear attack, but rather should develop a capability to deny to the Chinese the ability to inflict substantial damage on the United States. Part of this capability would come from highly accurate missile forces targeted on Chinese ICBM and bomber bases and capable of destroying these in a first strike if it was believed that China was about to launch a nuclear attack. However, because one can never be certain that the Chinese will not fire their missiles on warning or that the Chinese will not strike first, a damage denial capability requires an ABM system.

The desirability of a damage denial capability against China is sometimes expressed in terms of insurance. Advocates point out that one cannot be certain that the Chinese will not launch a nuclear attack. Even if the Chinese are not as belligerent and ignorant of the effects of nuclear war as is sometimes claimed, one cannot rule out a situation in which Chinese missiles would be launched against the United States. And a prudent man will buy insurance against this possibility.

Critics point out that insurance may not always be worth buying. If we can have high confidence that the Chinese will be deterred from nuclear attack, then the United States should not spend the $4 billion or $40 billion necessary to deploy an ABM system directed against China. Also, an ABM system against China might not work against a reasonably large Chinese attack. Weapon systems seldom work as planned the first time they are tested, and it is impossible to test realistically the Chinese-oriented ABM system before a Chinese attack.

Some advocates of a Chinese-oriented ABM system have argued that it is necessary for effective American diplomacy in the Far East. They suggest that as the Chinese develop an ICBM capability, Japan, Australia, and other countries will no longer believe that the United States will defend them against Chinese nuclear blackmail. Thus, particularly as the United States reduces its conventional forces in Asia, it has to develop a damage denial capability against China to maintain the credibility of the American deterrent and to maintain satisfactory relations with its Asian allies. Opponents of this view argue that just as the United States maintains the credibility of its deterrent in Europe despite the fact that the Soviet Union could destroy the United States, so it could maintain the credibility of its deterrent in the Far East. The Chinese would be deterred from nuclear threats or the use of nuclear weapons against American allies because they would recognize that the United States would respond with an overwhelming nuclear attack against China. America's allies, recognizing this, would continue to credit the reliability of the American deterrent even if China developed a small ICBM capability. Moreover, the Chinese could threaten to target Asian cities or American bases in the Far East, even if the United States built an ABM system.

Some critics of the Chinese-oriented ABM system argue that, although on its own terms it might be justified, one also has to take account of its impact on the Soviet Union. Because China and the Soviet Union are both north of the United States and missiles from the two countries would approach the United States through the same corridors, a ballistic-missile defense directed at China would pose a threat to the Soviet Union. The long lead time component of an ABM system is radar. In deploying a Chinese-oriented system, the United States would deploy all the large radar systems necessary against Soviet ICBMs. Thus a Chinese-oriented system would almost certainly force the Soviet Union to react by increasing the size of its strategic offensive forces. Critics argue that this disadvantage in terms of Soviet-American strategic interaction outweighs any possible gains with China. This would be particularly the case if it was possible in the Strategic Arms Limitation Talks with the Soviet Union to ban all ABM systems. If the Soviets could be prevented from deploying an ABM system that would threaten the American deterrent and in return could expect the United States to refrain from any ABM deployment, the price would be well worth paying even if it meant giving up possible advantages of an ABM system against China.

Some supporters of the effort to get a damage denial capability against China say that the United States should go further and seek a damage-limiting capability against the Soviet Union. They argue that the United States should deploy a large-area system to defend against a Soviet attack on American cities. They also favor developing highly accurate missiles that could destroy Soviet ICBMs and seeking to develop an antisubmarine warfare capability to track and destroy Soviet submarines. Proponents of this view reason that because the possibility of nuclear war could not be ruled out the United States should develop a capability to limit damage as far as possible in the event of a nuclear exchange with the Soviet Union.

It is also argued that this kind of capability would increase the political value of the American nuclear capability in deterring Soviet moves against America's allies.

Opponents of this position, including officials of the Nixon administration, argue that it is impossible to get an effective damage-limitation capability against the Soviet Union. Given the forces that the Soviet Union already has, it would be extremely expensive for the United States to deploy a capability to limit damage to any significant degree. Moreover, insofar as the United States actually developed a capability to limit damage, the Soviets would be forced to respond to maintain their own deterrent. The only result would be larger strategic forces on both sides, with larger expenditures without any significant damage-limiting capability for the United States.

Additional Sufficiency Issues

Several issues concerning strategic forces are not dealt with in the criteria for sufficiency put forward by the Nixon administration. One of these is the question of relative numbers. Throughout the 1960's the United States was ahead of the Soviet Union in almost all categories of strategic nuclear weapons. The United States had more bombers, intercontinental missiles, sea-based missiles, nuclear warheads, and greater accuracy and reliability. In 1970, when the Soviet Union deployed more fixed land-based missiles than the United States, the question came to the fore of whether the United States should permit the Soviet Union to gain a substantial advantage in any one category regardless of the effect on strategic sufficiency. Some feared that if the Soviet Union got substantially ahead in one or more areas, the Kremlin would be tempted to use this "superiority" for political advantage, perhaps in relation to Berlin. Others argued that as long as the United States had an effective deterrent a Soviet lead in one or more categories would make no difference.

A second issue not settled by the criteria for strategic sufficiency is how the United States should use its strategic forces in the event of a nuclear war. President Nixon's 1970 state of the world message suggested that he wished to have a capability other than that of retaliating by destroying Soviet cities. This raises a number of troublesome questions, which plagued the efforts during the McNamara era in the Pentagon to develop a controlled response capability. Among the difficulties is the need for a command and control system to ensure that strategic forces could be responsive to the wishes of political leaders. One step in this direction would be to deploy ABM systems to guard Washington and Moscow, increasing the probability that the two governments could negotiate an end to a strategic exchange rather than using all their forces.

Specific Weapon Decisions

No defense issue has raised more controversy in the United States in the postwar period than the question of whether the United States should deploy a ballistic-missile defense. A number of rationales have been advanced for an ABM system, and the determination of whether any of them makes sense can and must be treated as a separate question. However, much of the debate has focused on the general issue of whether the United States should deploy a ballistic-missile defense system of any kind. Before treating this overall question, we need to examine each of the possible roles of an ABM system.

One of these has already been discussed, that of damage denial against China. When Secretary of Defense McNamara first announced in September 1967 that the United States was deploying a ballistic-missile defense system, he described it as a Chinese-oriented system.

After ordering a reevaluation of the ABM question, President Nixon announced a reorientation of the ABM system. Although his *Safeguard* system is to be designed to provide protection against China, its first priority is protection of American fixed land-based missiles. The President noted that the increased accuracy of Soviet missiles and the possible deployment by the Soviet Union of MIRVs pose a threat to the *Minuteman* force. He pointed out that there are several ways of dealing with this problem. One is to move the missiles to new hard rock silos. A second possibility is to substitute a new strategic system, such as a mobile land-based missile. Another possibility is to simply increase the number of *Minuteman* missiles. Finally, he pointed out that there is the possibility of defending existing missiles with an ABM system. As the President suggested, one of the issues is whether this is the most effective way to ensure the survival of the land-based missile force. A second issue is whether the United States could abandon this system and rely on submarine-based forces and on strategic bombers. Even if one decides to defend the *Minuteman* missiles, there remains the question of whether the existing ballistic-missile defense system is capable of providing effective protection at a reasonable cost. In his statement in January 1970, Secretary of Defense Melvin Laird suggested that ballistic-missile defense of *Minuteman* missiles could be justified on cost-effectiveness grounds only if the United States was building an area defense for other purposes. He conceded that *Safeguard* radars were not optimum for *Minuteman* defense and were in fact extremely vulnerable to an enemy attack.

Another rationale for an ABM system is to provide a light area defense of the United States against small attacks. Such attacks might come from a power other than China or from the Soviet Union as a result of an accidental or unauthorized launch or following a large and successful American first strike. A light area defense system would protect the command and control system of the United States, particularly if reinforced with a local defense of Washington. Critics argue that a system kept operative at all times in order to have the possibility of shooting down a single missile would be extremely accident prone. However, if the system could be turned on only by the President, authority might not come before a missile had landed in the United States. They also raise the question as to whether it is worthwhile to spend $20 billion or $30 billion for defense against unlikely events.

For a number of years the Joint Chiefs of Staff advocated a large ABM system designed to defend the United States against a massive

Soviet attack. They argued that because the Soviets had built up a substantial missile capability and because ABM was technically feasible, the United States should deploy a large system. Such a system was estimated to cost from $15 billion to $20 billion, although experience with cost estimates suggests that the system would ultimately cost from $40 billion to $50 billion. Secretary of Defense McNamara, rejecting the Joint Chiefs' proposals for a large-area defense, argued that although the system would save American lives in a nuclear war against the existing Soviet threat, the Soviets could, with much less cost, respond and negate the effect of the large-area defense system. Both of his successors, Clark Clifford and Melvin Laird, have accepted this argument. President Nixon ruled out large-area defense against the Soviet Union not only because it was technically difficult but also because he proclaimed that it was not the policy of the United States to seek to take away the Soviet deterrent. A large-area defense that would threaten the Soviet deterrent would lead the Soviets to accelerate the arms race.

Most proponents and opponents of ABM systems have focused on the value of ABM for particular purposes, but in fact most of them have been for or against ABM as a whole. Those in favor of ABM see it as the natural evolution of technology. They argue that the United States must go forward with technological improvements that the Soviet Union is also working on and that the ABM system would provide a variety of advantages to the United States. Critics argue that the system would not work in any foreseeable situation, that it would accelerate the arms race, and that the United States should take a unilateral step to level off and end the nuclear arms race with the Soviet Union.

The Future of Land-based Missiles

The Nixon administration's focus on *Minuteman* defense as a rationale for the ABM system raises an issue that is likely to receive increasing attention in the next years. This is the question of whether the United States should continue to maintain fixed land-based missiles as part of its strategic force. As the Soviet Union improves the accuracy and reliability of its strategic missiles and as the number of its missiles increases, fixed land-based missiles will become increasingly vulnerable to a first strike. This process will be vastly accelerated if the Soviet Union develops accurate MIRV warheads. Thus, in looking ahead and being concerned about crisis stability, the Nixon administration has begun to consider the future of the land-based missile force. Its initial proposal was that these missiles be defended with the *Safeguard* ABM system. However, the technological limitations of that system have become increasingly apparent, and the Strategic Arms Limitation Talks could result in an agreement not to deploy a ballistic-missile defense.

If by agreement or unilaterally the *Safeguard* ABM system is ruled out, several alternatives would remain. One would be deployment of a new ABM system specifically designed for the local defense of *Minuteman*. A second would be deployment of mobile missiles. Mobile missiles might be placed on railroad cars or trucks and could be moved over a wide area, or they might simply move within a small area, back and forth on a track on a two-mile or five-mile radius. Another possibility is to move the missiles into special hard rock silos that would be considerably harder and more resistant to attack than the underground concrete silos currently protecting *Minuteman* missiles. However, these actions would only postpone the time when land-based missiles would be vulnerable to attack.

The final possibility would be for the United States to decide that it no longer needs to maintain three separate systems for deterrence. The United States would make no effort to protect its fixed land-based missiles and would phase them out when the Soviets developed a capability for an accurate attack against American missiles. At that time the United States would rely on sea-based missiles and on bombers.

CHAPTER EIGHT

LIMITED WAR: THE NATURE OF THE LIMITING PROCESS

The age of the nuclear missile has been characterized by warfare conducted without the use of modern nuclear weapons. Local wars — those that do not take place on the homelands of either the United States or the Soviet Union but still concern the two superpowers — have broken out from time to time in various parts of the globe. The process by which such wars start and by which the superpowers become involved yet refrain from using their major military capabilities is the subject of this chapter.

Determinants of Policy

Because the major powers have much more military force than they have used in any local war situation, an effort to understand the limiting process requires an examination of the decision-making procedures that determine to what extent the major powers will involve themselves in a local conflict. The determinants of this policy in terms of objectives, the fear of general war, images of the role of force, and domestic politics will be examined in turn.

Objectives. The general foreign policy objectives of the major powers influence their way of dealing with attempts by other powers or groups to bring about change by violent means. American foreign policy through the postwar period was guided by the objective of "containment." This meant in practice that the United States would attempt to use a combination of military, political, and economic pressures to prevent the expansion of Communist control, or control by the Soviet Union or China. The United States has also been committed to supporting the United Nations, with its ideal of employing peaceful methods for effecting change. The goal of the nonuse of military force has also been espoused by the United States. Finally, the United States has supported the objective of bringing about political stability and economic development in the non-Communist areas of the world.

The basic foreign policy objectives of the Soviet Union and China have been at considerable variance with American objectives, although there has been some change in the Soviet position over the last several years. Nevertheless, the Soviets appear to be interested in expanding the area under Soviet control and under Communist control, except where that expansion would give an important advantage to the Chinese. Peking remains committed to limiting American influence and military presence — first in Taiwan and then throughout Asia — and thereby expanding Chinese influence in the countries on the periphery. Throughout the world the Chinese have been interested in establishing revolutionary governments.

These broad political objectives, including more recent Soviet interest in international stability and containment of China, have shaped the way in which the major powers have looked upon particular attempts to change international boundaries or domestic political arrangements by the use of force. Nevertheless, partly because they are using only limited amounts of their military, political, and economic power, none of the superpowers can have any expectation of fulfilling all, or even a substantial part of, their general foreign policy objectives by conducting a local war. They are thus faced with the problem of relating their specific objectives to their more general and long-range aims.

Because of the relative lack of importance of the actual territories being fought over in limited-war situations, the most important objectives at stake have been the perceived political effects of various possible outcomes. In general, the superpowers have justified their intervention in local conflicts by citing the need to convince other countries that they would be defended if they came under attack. In reacting to the invasion of South Korea in 1950, to the Soviet ultimatums about Berlin in the late 1950's and early 1960's, to the Cuban missile crisis, and to the Vietcong threat in South Vietnam, the United States has been motivated — at least in part — by the belief that it could further deter Soviet or Chinese military moves only by intervening and thus establishing the credibility of its guarantee to other countries.

In many situations the United States has been more concerned with the lessons its allies and other countries would draw from its actions than with what was communicated to enemies. For example, American actions in Korea were carried out with an eye toward the reaction of Japan and America's NATO allies if South Korea had been allowed to fall. Similarly, the defense of South Vietnam has been justified on grounds that the Thais and others would accommodate China unless the United States showed in South Vietnam that it was prepared to defend them. This justification is sometimes discussed in terms of the "falling dominos" theory, which is based on the premise that if one country falls, all the other countries — at least in the area — would also fall to Communist control. Viewed mechanically and literally, the falling dominos image is obviously poor, but the fact that it would be harder for the United States to convince other allies of its commitment to defend them if the United States permitted one country to be taken by military violence seems clear. In any case, the calculation of political effects, in providing motivation for attempting to win a local war or at least for preventing the successful use of violence, has proved to be an important influence on American policymakers.

Other pressures have worked in the opposite direction. At least until 1965 the United States appeared to give the highest priority to the buildup of American and allied forces on the ground in Central Europe. It sought to use crises such as the Korean War to stimulate an increase in European defense efforts and was willing for this reason, and also because it feared that Korea might be a feint before Soviet attack in Europe, to increase substantially American strength in Europe while the Korean War was still going on. While all of America's allies are prepared to defend the principle that the United States should use force to prevent Communist takeovers, there has been much disagreement over specific uses of American military power. The war in Vietnam has generated much controversy not only in the United States but among America's allies. Some allied leaders have questioned American wisdom and proportion.

The objectives of the Soviet Union and China have been to create political effects that are the reverse of those sought by the United States. Thus, the two Communist powers are interested in demonstrating a general American weakness and lack of will or — in the words of the Chinese — that the United States is a "paper tiger" that must be tactically respected although strategically despised. Both the Soviets and the Chinese have also tried to demonstrate the power and capability of their countries; in particular, Peking has been committed to demonstrating the efficacy of supporting what it calls wars of national liberation.

The relationships between the political effects sought in fighting a locally limited war, the territorial objectives pursued, and the war-termination conditions that are acceptable have always been extremely difficult to calculate. As a result, there have been fluctuations and uncertainty in the war-termination conditions set by the superpowers. In the Korean War, for example, American objectives fluctuated all the way from defending South Korea to capturing all Korea, and the Soviets and Chinese were at one time seeking to capture all Korea and at another simply defending part of North Korea. Because a superpower tries to gauge, to some extent, contradictory reactions of various governments and peoples, there is no easy way of establishing the precise relation between one set of conditions terminating local war and another, and the political effects sought. Nevertheless, this attempt is made and determines the willingness of the superpowers to invest greater material effort to win a local war or leads them to seek an early termination of the conflict.

The Fear of General War. There is a widespread belief, apparently shared by leaders in the Soviet Union, the United States, and — despite their statements to the contrary — China, that the possibility of a general nuclear war increases during a local war. This fear — referred to in the West as the danger of "escalation" and by the Soviet Union as the danger of "a single spark" leading to a general nuclear war — has had a major impact on the decisions of the superpowers in relation to local wars and crises.

In examining the question of how a general nuclear war might arise from a local war, we must consider the two kinds of "escalation": expansion and explosion. In the process of expansion, local war — and this might especially apply to a local war in Europe — might increase gradually in size until, almost imperceptibly, it would become a general nuclear war involving attacks on the homelands of the Soviet Union and the United States. Alternatively, a local war, even a very low-level military clash, could suddenly explode into general nuclear war either because of fears of an inadvertent strike on both sides or because one side had deliberately decided to unleash nuclear war as a result of setbacks on the local battlefield.

The desire of the superpowers to avoid general nuclear war has been a major influence on the foreign policy of the United States, the Soviet Union, and China throughout the entire postwar period. Probably, leaders of these countries have had no clear image of how a general nuclear war might arise out of a local war, but they have recognized that the growing tension and increased use of military force could somehow get out of hand and lead to a nuclear conflict nobody wanted. They have realized that when decisions have to be made more quickly, when troops have to be authorized to make some decisions locally, and when tensions and political conflicts heighten, events may no longer be under the complete control of political leaders and may generate pressures leading to a nuclear war.

It is impossible to specify, either in general or for any historical event, how close the world actually has been to nuclear war or even just what it means to say that the world has moved closer to a nuclear war. Nevertheless, it appears that political leaders, because of the destructive nature of nuclear war, have tended to overestimate the probability that nuclear war would develop from any particular local crisis and, for that reason, have been less willing to commit military forces than they might otherwise be.

China, the United States, and the Soviet Union have all sought to manipulate the fear of general nuclear war in order to get advantages in a local conflict. However, with the exception of the Cuban missile crisis, there has been little explicit effort to exploit the particular nature of the strategic balance.

Images of the Role of Force. The way a country and its leaders look at international politics and their notions of what is proper behavior have an important impact on what policies they pursue and what actions they seek to prevent. In particular, images of the role that force can and should play in international politics influences the behavior of the United States, the Soviet Union, and China.

The United States is committed to the principle that force should not be used to settle political issues. Moreover, the United States believes that it has an obligation to prevent the use of force, particularly in changing international boundaries or the government of a country by outside military pressure. Virtually all American leaders — and certainly all who have been leaders since World War II — reject the notion that force should be used offensively by the United States to seek to change boundaries or alter control of governments. Although this principle has been violated on several occasions, there is a belief that only as much force as is necessary should be used to resist opposing forces.

Other ideas about the role of force have been widely held among dissenting American groups. Perhaps the most important of these is the belief that a clear moral and legal issue is needed to justify the use of violence. This range of concerns has influenced those who have criticized American involvement in Vietnam on the grounds that its legal and moral justifications are shaky and that the desire to prevent a Communist takeover in South Vietnam is simply not enough to overcome the restrictions that should be put on America's use of military force. At the other end are those that argue that the United States should intervene only if it is committed to "victory" — and at least in the early postwar period that meant victory over its major opponent. Thus, many objected to American conduct in the Korean War because the United States was committed to a "no-win" policy.

The Soviet Union and China, on the other hand, have looked upon force as a legitimate instrument of policy to be used interchangeably with other means in order to expand the area under Communist control. Furthermore, a belief in the importance of probing the enemy and testing his willingness to resist the use of force and in seeking to use as much force as can be successfully applied has evolved. Finally, the leaders of both countries have stressed the importance of political control over the use of military force.

Domestic Politics. There was a popular belief in the United States that politics should stop at the border, that there should be no domestic political conflict over foreign policy issues. Equally popular is the notion that in Communist societies foreign policy can be carried out without reference to domestic political considerations. In fact, however, domestic political considerations have played, and are likely to continue to play, a major role in determining policy on limited-war questions in the Soviet Union, China, and the United States. Although general war or even a large-scale conventional war could lead to the suspension of domestic political conflict, evidence from the Korean War and the war in Vietnam makes it clear that the conduct of a limited war would become an important domestic political issue and would be influenced by domestic political considerations. This is true, if for no other reason than that local wars require the use of scarce resources — resources that might otherwise be allocated for internal development or for other foreign policy activities. Therefore, the conduct of a war must be intimately related to general conflicts within the society about the correct and desirable allocation of resources. Certainly American policy in Vietnam has been heavily influenced by domestic pressures. From 1965 to 1968 the concern was mainly with pressures to escalate the conflict. Since then, President Johnson and President Nixon both have been influenced by the strong desire of many Americans to withdraw from South Vietnam. President Johnson's interest in promoting a Great Society influenced his actions as did Truman's interest in the Fair Deal. Similarly in the Soviet Union, and perhaps to a lesser extent in China, the proper role of the country in various local conflicts has been tied up with problems of succession and problems of policy.

The Limiting Process

The *limiting process* is the process by which local wars begin to settle on certain limits and are brought to an end. If a nuclear war begins, it will be because of the deliberate decision by one of a very few decision centers to use the weapons or at least to release them to troop commanders who can then make the decision to use them. Thus, deterrence of a general nuclear war can focus on decision-makers in Washington and Moscow. However, a local war can break out from a number of causes; it can result from the decisions of a large number of decision centers. Some of the local wars in the postwar period have erupted because of a deliberate decision by a Communist state to try to bring about change through the use of force. War in Korea, for example, resulted from a deliberate North Korean and Soviet decision. Or decisions made by groups in the local area — local Communist parties or local non-Communist groups or countries — may initiate local war. Finally, the United States might decide to begin a local war.

A local war is by definition limited. The limits that have been observed, and may be observed in future local wars, are of geography, targets, weapons, and the degree of participation of various states.

The geographic area in which local wars have been fought in the postwar period has been rather small; for example, the Korean War was limited to the Korean peninsula, the Cuban missile crisis to Cuba and the water surrounding it, the war in Vietnam to Indochina and the surrounding waters.

Even within the area of combat, both sides have observed limitations on targets attacked, particularly by airpower. The United States observed a series of different limitations during the Korean War. In the initial stages it attacked only military targets in North Korea; later it extended the area under attack to industrial targets, but not those close to the Soviet and Chinese borders. Then restrictions on attacks close to the Chinese border were removed. The Chinese, on the other hand, engaged in no bombing at all in South Korea except for some minor heckling raids. During the Vietnam War the United States has observed limitations on targets it would attack in North and South Vietnam.

Not using nuclear weapons has perhaps been the most significant limitation adhered to by the superpowers. The reasons for this restraint on the part of the United States and the Soviet Union have varied over time. One reason has been the belief that the use of nuclear weapons in a local conflict would make general nuclear war likely. A second reason is the belief that the use of these weapons would be extremely unpopular in other countries of the world. At the time of the Korean War, the United States had a relatively small supply of nuclear weapons and was inhibited by the desire not to use up forces that were seen as the major deterrent to possible Soviet moves elsewhere, particularly in Europe. There was also little understanding of the actual uses to which nuclear weapons could be put in tactical situations. Neither the United States nor the Soviet Union now have any real shortage of nuclear capability, and both have developed much more sophisticated nuclear weapons of various sizes and effects. Nevertheless, the political costs of using nuclear weapons seem even greater than before, as does the danger that the use of nuclear weapons will make general war likely.

Other limitations on weapons have been observed by various countries in particular limited wars. No countries have, for example, used lethal biological or chemical weapons; and the Chinese Communists and Soviets have refrained from introducing various kinds of weaponry, including submarines and bombers, into a number of limited-war situations.

The degree of participation of the superpowers in any local-war situation varies from virtual indifference or failure to take sides, as the Soviets did during the Indo-Pakistani clash in 1965, to direct involvement of combat troops, for example, on the part of the United States in Korea and Vietnam. The points in between can range from active diplomatic aid, through the sending of military supplies and technicians, through the use of volunteers or advisers in a more active combat role.

Can any general statements be made about why limited wars take the course they actually do, why certain limits are observed, and why war terminates in the way that it does?

Perhaps the most important generalization is: The specifics of any limited-war situation will determine the direction of that encounter. The explanation for any limited war is to be seen less as a consequence of some general propositions about limiting war in the nuclear age than as a result of specific international and local political factors.

Limits are carried out not because of any agreement, whether tacit or formal, between the countries concerned, but because of decisions made within various countries. Therefore, to understand limited war we must look not only at the interaction between states but also at the internal decision-making processes.

Events since 1949 have demonstrated repeatedly what many analysts continued to doubt into the 1950's — namely, that limited wars were possible, that superpowers, whether democracies or dictatorships, could be involved in military conflicts with significant numbers of casualties and still refrain from attacking the homeland of the opposing superpower. Limiting their involvement has also included stopping somewhere short of the use of their major weapons systems and stopping in a way that does not force their opponent to use all its military power.

The limits that have been observed result from domestic decision-making processes; these limits can be catalogued from an international perspective. It is clear that some of them are symmetrical: both sides refrain from doing the same things. Some may even result from conscious bargaining and interaction. However, many are not symmetrical: one side refrains from doing something the other side is doing. And many are not based on any conscious bargaining process or recognition of likely reactions. Many limits are actually based on misunderstandings, misconceptions, or at least different perceptions of what is taking place. Others may be based on negotiating and bargaining with allies or with other countries rather than with the enemy.

The initiation of a local conflict is frequently not deliberate; certainly fighting is not always started because of a deliberate decision by one of the superpowers. A local conflict may also be terminated for reasons unrelated to the interest of the superpowers and frequently for reasons unrelated to the local battlefield outcome.

Finally, it is difficult to judge who wins a local war. If both sides are fighting mainly because of the political effects of winning or losing, these questions become relevant: What are the political effects in specific situations, and how might they be changed by additional efforts on the battlefield? The answers to these questions plague historians and political analysts as much as they do policymakers. What, for example, would have been the consequences of permitting North Korea to overrun South Korea or, on the other hand, the consequences of carrying the war to China and capturing all North Korea? What would be the consequences of permitting Quemoy or even Berlin to be taken over by the Communists? What did the United States gain from the successful defense of Quemoy in 1958? These are difficult questions to answer, even in retrospect, and were much more difficult to deal with at the time. Because of these uncertainties, because there are no clear answers, the decisions taken by various countries will be affected by a range of factors — some directly relevant to the situation, some not. A general understanding of the limiting process is useful for considering particular situations and determining policy for the direct defense of local areas, but it is only a small part of what we need to know.

CHAPTER NINE

DETERRENCE AND DEFENSE IN EUROPE

The NATO alliance was formed in 1949 because of the belief that the Soviet Union might attempt a military move in Central Europe within the next few years. There had been a widespread fear that such an attack would occur during the time of the Berlin blockade in 1948, and these fears were expressed again following the outbreak of the Korean War in June 1950. During the early years of the alliance all members shared the views that war was extremely likely, that it could be deterred only by a substantial buildup of alliance forces, and that one had to be ready to fight. During the 1950's the belief in the imminence of war in Europe declined slowly but steadily, so that by the end of the decade war in Europe was thought extremely unlikely. Many attributed this change to the military strength of NATO; therefore, it seemed necessary to maintain this force and to develop a strategy consistent with the belief that although war in Europe was improbable the residual possiblity of war did exist.

At the same time, increased attention was given to the problems of political relations within the alliance. By the late 1960's, most NATO countries were more concerned with détente — efforts to improve relations with the Soviet Union — than with defense. The problem of deterring, or defending against, a Soviet military attack is dealt with in this chapter.

The Soviet Military Threat

Though all forms of military action in the NATO area are believed to be unlikely, it is recognized that history consists of the occurrence of the unlikely and, in many cases, the occurrence of unforeseen events; therefore, the forces of the NATO alliance plan for various contingencies. This planning begins with an attempt to assess the range of possible Soviet military threats. The most serious, also perhaps the most improbable, Soviet threat would be the initiation of large-scale ground war on the central front. An all-out attack on the central front, a Soviet attempt to reach the English Channel as quickly as possible — this image of warfare guided the formation of NATO but has come to seem unrealistic. Short of an all-out attack, the Soviets might use their forces for a probe — an attempt to discover whether NATO would be willing to react militarily — perhaps by seizing a piece of territory. Such a probe could conceivably occur on the central front (most probably in Berlin but possibly in other cities such as Hamburg), on the northern front on the northern cap of Norway, or on the southern front in the area of Greece and Turkey.

Moving down the scale of violence from the overt use of military force, the Soviets have employed their military capability for political purposes. They have engaged in some limited forms of nuclear blackmail — for example, threatening to destroy any airbase from which an American U-2 plane took off. They might engage in more drastic acts of nuclear blackmail, such as ordering a country to withdraw from the NATO alliance or to suffer the consequence — a nuclear attack. Short of this blackmail, the Soviets have used the presence of their large military forces in Central Europe as a form of military pressure and have affected political discussions about the future of Central Europe. Following their invasion of Czechoslovakia in 1968, the Soviets appeared to be threatening military action against countries in the zone between the NATO and Warsaw Pact countries. In particular the Yugoslavian government expressed concern. These events raised the question of whether NATO has a role to play in protecting countries such as Sweden, Yugoslavia, Austria, and Finland, which were not members of NATO but had close political, cultural, and economic ties with the West. Finally, the Soviets have employed their military force on their own side of the iron curtain: their large-scale efforts occurred in 1956, when Soviet troops squelched the Hungarian revolution and in 1968 when the Soviets invaded Czechoslovakia. There appears to be a tacit understanding that NATO will not interfere in cases of military action in Eastern Europe.

The Soviet Union has restricted itself to low-level military actions; it will probably continue to do so. However, more severe actions, if carried out, would result in great cost to the West. Thus NATO has to decide what threats it wants to be able to deal with and how it will deal with them.

Must NATO prepare for events perceived to be extremely unlikely? Some Europeans and Americans, viewing any military action in Central Europe as improbable, conclude that only small military forces are needed in Europe; others argue that a Soviet limited probe, such as an attempt to seize Hamburg, is even more unlikely and less worth preparing for. There is also the question of how far NATO interests extend. Do they extend, for example, to Sweden or to the countries of Eastern Europe?

What threats are to be met is related to the appropriate strategies for dealing with threats — what contingencies are likely to occur and the cost involved in preparing for them.

Alternative NATO Strategies

Strategies proposed for the defense of the NATO area include massive retaliation, the instant use of tactical nuclear weapons, the pause, and conventional defense. These strategies have generally been considered in terms of their effectiveness in deterring an attack on the central front. However, our assumption is that it is necessary to consider these alternatives not only in relation to deterrence but also in terms of a failure of deterrence and the use of military force needed. The economic and domestic political costs of various strategies for different countries must also be weighed.

Massive Retaliation. The strategy of massive retaliation is based on the threat of instant and massive use of strategic nuclear power by the West, particularly that of the United States against the Soviet Union in the event of Soviet aggression in Europe. This strategy, which was the basis of NATO planning — at least until 1954 when the emphasis was put on tactical nuclear weapons — requires no ground forces for its implementation. Because the strategic nuclear power is to be used immediately against the Soviet Union, there appears to be no need for forces that would directly defend against Soviet attack. Nevertheless, it has always been argued that some ground troops are needed. In the earliest postwar years there was some doubt as to whether the nuclear power of the alliance was sufficient to quell a Soviet attack. It was believed that even after all American weapons — what by current standards was a limited stock — had been used, the Soviet Army might continue to advance. Even after this no longer seemed possible, because of the large strategic stockpile belonging to the United States, some ground troops seemed necessary to establish the fact that aggression had taken place. Terms such as "plate-glass window" and "trip-wire" were used to express the notion that troops on the ground, including American troops, would signal that aggression had, in fact, taken place. The enemy would be forced to destroy these troops, thus "breaking the glass" or "tripping the wire" and bringing into play the American strategic force. Finally, and perhaps most important, the presence of American ground troops in Europe has been considered necessary to affirm the political guarantee of the United States. The American military divisions in Europe are a way of providing a hostage force to demonstrate the American commitment to Europe and to make more credible the use of nuclear weapons by the United States in the defense of

Europe. Consequently, if the United States were to station large numbers of troops on the central front, it was believed necessary to have a corresponding number of European ground troops, even if the purpose of the American troops was largely to symbolize the American commitment.

The threat of the use of massive strategic nuclear weapons seems to have in fact been sufficient, if not necessary, to deter a full-scale Soviet attack on the central front. The Soviets may never have planned such an attack, but even if they had at least contemplated such action, the possibility that it would lead to a general nuclear war was probably sufficient in the past and will remain sufficient in the future to deter the attack. However, the threat of massive retaliation has proved unsuccessful and unsatisfactory in dealing with lesser threats, including the various Soviet moves against Berlin.

Clearly, the strategy of massive retaliation would be unsatisfactory if deterrence failed. If war did break out in Europe — either because of a deliberate Soviet decision on the assumption that American military power would not be used or if a large-scale war were to grow out of, for example, an uprising in East Germany — massive retaliation would not be the desired strategy to use. Once war began, some alternative options to the strategic nuclear power of the alliance would be needed. Few, if any, commentators or officials consider massive retaliation an acceptable action policy, and only a small number consider it even a satisfactory communication policy. Thus, there has been a search for alternatives that would provide for ground forces in Europe for dealing with at least the initial stages of a Soviet attack.

Tactical Nuclear Weapons. In the mid-1950's the United States began to develop an arsenal of sophisticated and varied tactical nuclear weapons. At the same time it had become evident that the countries of the NATO alliance were not going to deploy the number of ground divisions believed necessary to deal directly with a Soviet threat. Thus, as the fear that nuclear weapons alone would not be sufficient to deter the Soviet Union gave way to the belief that relying on strategic nuclear weapons only was not the most advisable plan, tactical nuclear weapons became the only solution. This strategy, adopted formally by the NATO Council in 1957, called for ground forces of significant size, perhaps thirty divisions on the central front, equipped with tactical nuclear weapons. Planning was based on the assumption that the use of these weapons would be authorized immediately if an attack occurred; thus, planning was only for tactical or strategic nuclear war.

This strategy continues to be favored by most NATO military planners. It assumes that any action on the central front would be a major military move deliberately taken by the Soviet Union and hence an action significant enough to justify the introduction of nuclear weapons by the West. It assumes also that it is clearly to the advantage of the West to use tactical nuclear weapons in the event of local ground warfare. This question has been debated widely with inconclusive results, but there is a growing consensus that the use of tactical nuclear weapons is not necessarily an advantage to the West nor does it reduce the manpower needed to deal with a given enemy force. Some analysts, however, argue that the use of nuclear weapons is an advantage to the West, that the West has and will continue to have a substantial lead in the development of tactical nuclear weapons and hence can fight effectively with them. Those who advocate a tactical nuclear defense of Europe tend to share some of these views about the advantage of using nuclear weapons and take one of two attitudes toward a conventional defense. They either argue that it is impossible, given the large Soviet conventional forces, or they argue that emphasis on conventional forces is undesirable because they reduce the credibility of the deterrent value of nuclear weapons and make war more likely.

In order to come to grips with the question of the value of tactical nuclear weapons, it is necessary to examine several views of what a tactical nuclear war might be like. In the following four models of tactical nuclear war in Europe, the use of these weapons increases.

The first model is the use of tactical nuclear weapons essentially in a warning or so-called shot-across-the-bow role. It assumes that any use of nuclear weapons would lead quickly to large-scale nuclear war or to peace. Therefore, the small-scale use of these weapons, carrying the threat of explosion into general nuclear war, would lead both sides to agree quickly to halt military operations. The advocates of this strategy believe that in the event of an outbreak of military operations, NATO should order the firing of a single nuclear weapon or successive ones to demonstrate its resolve, seriousness, and willingness to risk general nuclear war. Some advocates of this strategy argue that this single shot should be directed at a tactical military target in the area of operations. Others contend that it should be directed at an industrial or economic target, either in Eastern Europe or perhaps in the Soviet Union. As a result of the analysis of tactical nuclear war in the NATO Nuclear Planning Group, the British and West German governments have apparently come to support this approach to the use of tactical nuclear weapons. They appear to have accepted this view after rejecting alternative approaches because of the great damage it would do.

The success of this strategy depends on two assumptions, both of which are doubtful. The first is that the resolve of the NATO alliance will be stronger than that of the Soviet Union. It is difficult to believe, however, that once an action that increases the risk of nuclear war has been taken, the bargaining position of the NATO alliance will cause the Soviet Union to be more willing to negotiate on reasonable terms than it was before the nuclear weapon was used. The strategy assumes also that the negotiation, regardless of the resolve of the two parties, could settle on something other than the status quo on the battlefield and specifically that it could settle on a return to the status quo ante. However, in a situation in which the pressure to negotiate stems from the belief that general nuclear war is about to break out, it appears extremely doubtful that one can negotiate a return to the status quo ante. In fact, the use of nuclear weapons to demonstrate resolve may most likely lead to a breakup of the NATO alliance and a willingness on the part of some countries to settle on terms that seem disastrous to others.

A second model of tactical nuclear war assumes that the use of nuclear weapons would be confined to low-yield, subkiloton weapons and to the immediate battlefield area. In such a case, civilian casualties could be held at relatively low levels, not significantly higher than those of a conventional war. However, the effect on the battlefield is largely uncertain. The use of such weapons, for example, may make offensive breakthroughs much easier. In general, in a conventional war it is believed that one must have a superiority of approximately three to one in a particular area in order to make a major advance on the ground. The use of tactical nuclear weapons could substitute for conventional firepower and make breakthroughs possible with much smaller ratios of offensive to defensive forces. The use of such weapons could also lead to a total collapse of the armies in the field, resulting in a freezing of the status quo, at the time at which tactical nuclear weapons are used. If both sides fear the introduction of tactical nuclear weapons, strong urges to launch an inadvertent strike are likely to develop both locally and throughout the theater or area of battle because the first use of these weapons could succeed in destroying large numbers of troops and equipment not protected against the possibility of a nuclear attack. Forces ready for nuclear attack would have to be more effectively protected. This instability not only increases the probability that tactical nuclear weapons might be introduced but also forces troops fighting conventionally to consider at least the need to fight in a way that assumes that tactical nuclear weapons may be used at any time.

A tactical nuclear war fought with low-yield weapons confined to the battlefield would be extremely unstable. Pressures to expand the war by using larger weapons from beyond the battlefield and attacking logistics lines leading into the battlefield would probably be great and, if yielded to, could result in enemy attacks on these weapons systems — on the airbases and missile sites from which weapons are being launched into battle. These actions could quickly result in the theater use of nuclear weapons.

Those who believe that a tactical nuclear war might be confined to small weapons and that such a war is in any case worth preparing for are still faced with the problem of what kinds of nuclear weapons would be most effective in a narrow, tactical, military sense for such an encounter and which weapons would be most effective in preventing the expansion of the tactical nuclear war. A number of studies have been conducted attempting to answer these questions, but the essential uncertainties stemming from the fact that there has never been a tactical nuclear war have made it impossible to develop any consensus on these questions.

In the third model tactical nuclear war would involve the use of much larger nuclear weapons, including weapons in the megaton weight range, over the whole theater of military operations. Nuclear weapons may initially be introduced on this scale or after the battlefield use of nuclear weapons. Such a use would mean many civilian casualities, virtually equaling the complete destruction and devastation of Europe. The use of nuclear weapons on this scale is proposed mainly as a deterrent and not as an action policy for that NATO alliance.

In the final model the assumption is made that any war in Europe would lead automatically to worldwide nuclear war in which theater operations — even theater operations in Europe — would not be critical and in which the focus of action would be the strategic interchange between the United States and the Soviet Union.

The Pause. During the late 1950's a number of NATO strategists, including the Supreme Allied Commander in Europe, General Lauris Norstad, began to be uneasy about strategies that called for the early introduction of tactical nuclear weapons. These strategists feared on the one hand that the authorization to use nuclear weapons would not come quickly enough to permit the implementation of the strategy and on the other that the use of tactical nuclear weapons would not necessarily be to the advantage of the West. Because of the delay in getting the political authority to use nuclear weapons, it was argued that a pause would inevitably take place, that there would be a period of time during which the West would try to hold the Soviet advance with conventional weapons before nuclear weapons would be used. This question was raised: If some delay was inevitable, should this delay be lengthened so that it would exceed the time necessary to get authority to use nuclear weapons and would be measured in hours or even days during which an end to the fighting could be negotiated?

The strategy assumes that war breaks out either through accident or inadvertence or because of Soviet miscalculation of NATO intentions. Implicit in this strategy, then, is the belief that if the use of nuclear weapons can be delayed for several days, the use will no longer be necessary. However, even in these cases the pause strategy raises a number of questions. Negotiations during a pause, like those following a shot-across-the-bow use of tactical nuclear weapons, are likely to lead at best to a freezing of the status quo at the current battle lines. In both cases the Soviets will be in a strong position, knowing that the West will be faced at the end of the period with the choice of defeat or a large-scale use of tactical nuclear weapons. The pause has a built-in deadline: after the period the NATO alliance must use nuclear weapons, which it has demonstrated a reluctance to use, or face the collapse of its conventional troops. In this situation, negotiations may well lead to a breakup of the alliance over peace terms or over the proper way to use nuclear weapons, resulting in increased Soviet strength.

The decision to introduce nuclear weapons after a pause assumes that, in general, introduction of these weapons would help the West, in which case it is not clear why they have not been used from the outset, at least as soon as permission could be obtained. In any case, there is great uncertainty and great danger of explosion into general nuclear war. The use of battlefield weapons after Soviet advances during the period of a pause is most likely to freeze Soviet gains. Finally, the theater use of nuclear weapons can be most profitable before the Soviets bring up reinforcements; that is, the use of these weapons in an interdictory role to cut off Soviet supplies of troops and ammunition appears to be most effective. Once substantial numbers of Soviet reinforcements have been brought up, it is not certain that even the use of excessive numbers of nuclear weapons would be of value to the West.

Conventional Defense. Dissatisfactions with strategies that rely on the use of tactical nuclear weapons led to a growing interest, at least in the United States, in strategies that depend to some extent on the use of conventional weapons, and in 1968 NATO adopted a flexible response strategy, which included a conventional defense component. The new NATO strategy requires that NATO forces be equipped and trained for conventional wars of significant duration. This is a substantial change from NATO doctrine of the 1950's and the first half of the 1960's, for then NATO forces were not trained or equipped for conventional war. Airplanes did not have conventional bomb racks; pilots were not trained for conventional operations; artillery pieces of the right kind did not exist; airplanes were not protected against conventional attack. A flexible response strategy assumes that NATO would try to convince the Soviets that the alliance would respond to any attack but that its response might initially be conventional, reserving the right to use nuclear weapons. NATO in fact seems to intend to respond to some kinds of conventional attack by conventional means. This strategy assumes that the deterrent, insofar as it depends on military force at all, depends primarily on convincing the Soviets that there will be a NATO response, including an American response. Deterrence depends much less on the form of military response than it does on the certainty of a response. Therefore, a certain conventional response to conventional aggression is a more credible tactical deterrent than the threat of a nuclear response.

There appears to be a consensus within NATO about the advisability of some form of flexible response strategy, including a conventional defense capability. Dispute concerns how large the conventional force should be, and this depends on the contingencies NATO should be prepared to respond to with conventional forces, evaluation of the threat, and determination of force requirements to meet a given contingency.

Some argue that NATO should have a conventional capability against only small attacks — accidental or limited probes or unintended engagements that might come up quickly. Thus NATO's conventional capability would consistent of the ability to rapidly deploy four or five divisions to the central front or to the northern or southern flank. Those who argue that this is the only conventional capability that NATO should have have several views about a larger conventional defense. Many of them have argued that it is not politically feasible. Given the politics of the NATO alliance, the domestic politics of NATO countries, and the existence of a large Soviet force — which means that a major conventional defense would require a large increase in NATO conventional capabilities — it is impossible for NATO to have a conventional capability against large attacks.

Some have argued that NATO does not need a major conventional capability because the threat of all-out conventional war is so low that spending money to prepare for this contingency is simply not worthwhile. Others assert that conventional capability is irrelevant because Soviet military doctrine would lead the Soviets to use nuclear weapons in any large-scale war. And finally some have reasoned that a substantial conventional capability would reduce the deterrent against Soviet attack. If the Soviets became convinced that NATO might fight a large conventional war without using nuclear weapons, the danger of a large conventional war would increase. What deters the Soviets, according to this view, is the knowledge that NATO would use nuclear weapons if the war got big.

Another view is that NATO should prepare for conventional defense against the entire range of possible conventional attacks. Those who hold this opinion argue that, although small attacks are most likely, diplomacy is most affected by the shadow of the overall military balance, and therefore to be able to resist Soviet diplomatic moves and to facilitate its own diplomatic efforts NATO should have a full range of conventional capabilities, including mobilization to deal with Soviet mobilization. Proponents of this view declare that it is feasible because the Soviet threat has been greatly exaggerated. There is now a rough military balance between NATO and the Warsaw Pact, and the need is for marginally improving conventional capabilities and not for spending vast sums. Although an all-out Soviet attack is extremely unlikely, the consequences of resorting to nuclear weapons to resist such an attack will be so great and so unpleasant that it is worth paying to have the option of conventional defense. It is possible that the Soviets will begin a large attack with nuclear weapons, but it is possible too that they will not, and this contingency is worth preparing for. Also, NATO would be unlikely to use a small local conventional capability if it knew that if the war grew beyond that size it would be forced to use nuclear weapons. Only if NATO could match Soviet conventional capabilities over the spectrum of contingencies and over time would there be any possibility that NATO would in fact commit small conventional forces to limited operations.

Another question affecting the necessary size of NATO conventional forces concerns the Soviet threat. How effective are Soviet forces? How many men could the Soviets deploy after thirty or ninety days of mobilization? How good are their tanks and planes compared to those of NATO? These enormously complicated and highly controversial questions have no clear answers.

Beginning in 1961, the Kennedy administration undertook its own intensive effort to reevaluate these questions and proposed to have NATO study the military balance. In 1969 the Nixon administration launched an intensive effort within the American government to determine the military balance in Central Europe and then asked for a NATO study. Other NATO members have carried on their own studies, and the alliance as a whole annually examines the military balance.

There continues to be a very wide range of opinion, extending from the position taken by the Office of Systems Analysis in the Department of Defense during the 1960's that there was a rough balance in military force in Central Europe, to the view that continues to be expressed by NATO military commanders that there is an enormous Soviet advantage in conventional military power. These differences result partly from different bureaucratic interests and different political objectives but also from the fact that there simply are no agreed-upon analytic methods for determining the size of military forces and their relative effectiveness. In the end, war is an art, not a science.

There is also the question of what confidence one needs to do what against various threats. One view is that one must be certain of success; that is, if NATO policy is to have the capability for conventional defense against all conventional attacks, then NATO must be certain of success in all contingencies. There is another way of looking at the problem, and that is to recognize that what is at issue is deterrence and, because deterrence is in the eye of the beholder, force requirements should be stated in terms of enemy perceptions rather than in terms of conservative calculations by the defender. NATO forces should have the ability to deny the Soviet Union any confidence of success in an attack using the forces it maintains in Eastern Europe, the capability to deny the Soviets any high confidence in success following a secret, rapid mobilization, and a mobilization capability for the Europeans and a reinforcement capability for the United States so that the alliance could deny the Soviet Union confidence of success at any stage in the process of mobilization and reinforcement that might occur during a crisis in Europe.

CHAPTER TEN

DETERRENCE AND DEFENSE IN ASIA

Military strategists have devoted most of their attention to general war problems and to NATO issues. Much less has been written about problems of deterrence and defense in Asia. Moreover, there is no single problem of Asian security, and most of the important issues are as much political as they are military. This chapter is a consideration of some of the strategic issues that affect American security policy in Asia.

Nuclear Weapons for Deterrence and Defense

The role of any weapon systems in deterrence must be considered in relation to the countries or groups against which the deterrent threat is directed and the actions of the group that are to be deterred. The image of the United States confronting a monolithic Communist bloc consisting of the Soviet Union, China, small Communist states in Asia and Europe, as well as Communist parties united and taking direction from a single leader in Moscow, has been effectively shattered by the events of the last decade. It is now clear that the United States confronts a variety of Communist threats. This is not to say that the Communist states might not align with each other in certain situations and under certain pressures from the United States or that they might not even coordinate some offensive actions. Rather, a credible threat against one center of Communist power — for example, Moscow — is no longer sufficient (assuming that it ever was) to deter actions by Peking, not to speak of those of North Vietnam or the Indonesian Communist Party. Thus, in seeking to assess the role of deterrence in Asia, we must distinguish between deterrent threats directed at the Soviet Union, those directed at China, those directed at other Communist parties in power (North Vietnam and North Korea), and those directed at Communist insurgency groups or political parties in countries such as Indonesia and South Vietnam. It is obvious that the problems in each case will be different. A threat to bomb Hanoi, for example, may look much less threatening to China than to the North Vietnamese and perhaps even less threatening to Moscow. On the other hand, threats of massive retaliation directed against the Soviet homeland may appear unreal, incredible, and not operative for local Communist forces.

All the possible sources of violence and aggression in Asia do not stem from communism. The United States is interested in deterring military action between various states in Asia, including India, Pakistan, Malaysia, Indonesia, South Vietnam, and Cambodia. In none of these cases has the United States sought to bring into play its nuclear deterrent capability.

In determining situations in which deterrent threats may be effective, another factor to be considered is what actions are to be deterred. In the Asian theater, violence has taken a great variety of forms ranging from rioting and political assassination through wars of national liberation to conventional wars. In addition, the United States has sought to deter the possibility of the expansion of a conventional war to a war using nuclear weapons. Finally, as the military power of China grows, the United States will want to be in a position to counter the political effect of Chinese threats of nuclear blackmail, as it has dealt with Soviet threats.

A pairing-off of the various kinds of actions with the countries or groups being deterred provides a wide range of possibilities.

However, for most of these, nuclear deterrence has not been used and appears to be irrelevant. For some, such as a Soviet nuclear attack on Japan, the efficacy of nuclear deterrence seems obvious enough so that a separate treatment is not necessary. The most important problems will occur in relation to the deterrence of China from actions ranging from support for wars of national liberation through conventional war and various efforts to exploit China's growing nuclear capability. The role of American nuclear and conventional power in deterring or defending against such Chinese actions is complex.

In discussions of the European situation, it is often said that there is no way of telling if deterrence works because it is not known whether the Soviet Union has contemplated military action. Some assert that clearly deterrence has worked because there has been no military action. Either way this problem is approached, deterrence has not "worked" in Asia. Despite the vast preponderance of American power, which was even greater in earlier periods, Communist countries have engaged in a number of acts of military violence across international boundaries in the Far East. There are, then, a series of actions that have been taken in the past and might be taken in the future by Communist groups in Asia, including China, which might be called undeterrable actions — that is, actions that fall below any ability of the United States to effectively bring its nuclear power to bear.

Thus far in the postwar period, Chinese undeterrable actions have fallen into four categories:

1. *Conventional military action.* This has occurred beyond what the Chinese claim to be their international borders only once, at the time of the Chinese intervention in the Korean War. Even at the time of the intervention, the Chinese were influenced by American atomic power. There have been no signs of even a threat of this kind of conventional intervention by the Chinese since 1950, and it appears that such action will continue to be deterred and is, in fact, now in the "overdeterred" category.

2. *Conventional military action within "Chinese territory."* The

major military adventure by the Chinese Communists in the post-war period was the invasion of Tibet in 1950. This has been followed by continuous effort to suppress Tibetan revolts. Chinese action there was taken with the notion that Tibet was indisputably part of China. The reaction of the United States to the event, including failure to ask for General Assembly condemnation, indicated that the United States took a similar view of the action. The Chinese have a completely free hand in running Tibet and are continuing to suppress the minor Tibetan attempts to throw the Chinese out. It seems unlikely that any American nuclear or conventional power would be brought to bear in this kind of situation.

3. *Border probes.* Chinese probes around their borders have been concentrated mainly against India and in the Taiwan Straits against the offshore islands, which the Chinese consider to be part of their own territory. In these cases the action has been limited and of relatively short duration. To some extent, action has been explicitly designed to fall below the American nuclear threshold — that is, it has been sufficiently limited so that the United States would not respond with nuclear weapons.

These events are undeterrable only in the sense that the Chinese can always find some low-level military pressure that will be below the threshold of nuclear deterrence. However, how much probing they could expect to get away with, without running the risk of provoking American nuclear threats, can only be surmised.

4. *Support for wars of national liberation.* The major Chinese action here has been in support of actions in the Indochinese peninsula. Again the degree of support rendered by the Chinese could be affected by nuclear threats, but it seems likely that there would remain a degree of activity that would not run any risk of bringing on a nuclear attack against China. The basic Chinese position is that foreign governments can lend only moral support, train guerrillas, and give limited military aid. These actions appear unlikely to provoke an American nuclear attack.

At the other end of the spectrum, there are situations that appear to be "overdeterred"; as in Europe, there are an abundance of political and military incentives working against aggression. Where Europe and Asia differ in this regard, however, is in the conventional capabilities of the opposing sides. At times in the postwar period, the Soviet Union did have conventional superiority in Europe. Such superiority on the part of the Communist bloc in Asia existed, if at all, only in the early months of 1950, when the American Army remained almost entirely a potential military force. There is no doubt now, however, that for the foreseeable future conventional military power is sufficient to defeat and, consequently, to deter a Chinese Communist effort to invade any of the islands off the mainland of Asia — among others, Japan, Taiwan, the Philippines, and Indonesia. Conventional power also appears to be adequate to defeat and to deter a Chinese attempt to invade India or to reinvade South Korea. It is difficult to assess the role that nuclear deterrence plays in these situations. American nuclear power is probably sufficient by itself to prevent a Chinese Communist attack against Japan, India, Taiwan, Malaysia, and the others, while, on the other hand, conventional power alone is sufficient to deter these actions. Finally, it remains uncertain whether, even barring sufficient conventional and nuclear capability, the Chinese would have been tempted to undertake military moves, except against Taiwan. We can say that as long as the United States has any nuclear force, it will play a role in deterring Chinese military moves. But the United States could depend, both in its planning and in its deterrent statements, on the threat of a conventional response.

The "deterred" is what lies in between the "undeterrable" and the "overdeterred" — that is, actions China might well have contemplated in the postwar period but which were deterred by American nuclear capability. No attempt can be made to be exhaustive about this category because we are dealing with what is essentially unknown — unknown perhaps even to Peking. The Communists came to power in China after the United States had developed nuclear weapons; consequently, they have always had to assess their foreign policy opportunities in relation to American superiority in nuclear weapons. There may be certain tactics and certain objectives that have never come to the fore but that might have if the United States had not possessed a nuclear capability or had not seemed willing to use it in Asia under certain circumstances.

Chinese Communist moves in the Taiwan Straits, particularly against the offshore islands of Quemoy and Matsu, appear to fall within the category of deterred actions. It is difficult to make any general assessment of the possibility of conventional defense of the offshore islands. However, given America's relative neglect of conventional capability in the late 1950's, it seems possible that there were at least some periods during which Quemoy could have been captured in spite of an American and Chinese Nationalist conventional defense. In any event, Peking might have tried further moves against the offshore islands in the absence of an American nuclear capability. It is also possible, but by no means certain, that further moves against India might have taken place in the absence of an American nuclear capability.

The Chinese might also have been willing to increase their involvement in particular local conflicts if the American nuclear threat had not been present. They might have fought longer in Korea; they might have pressed further during the 1958 Quemoy crisis; and they might well at the moment be giving increased aid to North Vietnam were it not for the fear of an American nuclear attack against China.

It is argued, then, that there are some events in a middle range, where American nuclear power may play a critical role, although this middle range is difficult to define. Nevertheless, it is felt that this range is bounded on one side by actions the United States has not at any time been able to deter and, on the other, by actions that seem overdeterred.

The Chinese are developing a nuclear capability at least partly to be in a position in which they can deter more effectively an American nuclear attack. In fact — and the Chinese appear to recognize this fact — the United States may be more likely to use nuclear weapons against China now that China has begun to develop its own nuclear capability; in this situation, the United States would be using nuclear weapons against a nuclear power that, at least implicitly, was threatening to use its own nuclear weapons in the area of local conflict. In addition, Chinese nuclear installations provide an obvious target for a limited American nuclear attack. Thus, in the current period, the Chinese may be expected to be even more cautious, and the range of deterrable actions may extend even further.

As the Chinese develop a nuclear delivery capability directed initially at Asian cities, their confidence in their ability to deter American intervention is likely to increase. It will increase even further when they have the ability to attack the United States. The Chinese may then be willing to probe the limits of the undeterrable; that is, they may increase their support of wars of national liberation in Asia and may begin to probe along their own borders, perhaps again in the Taiwan Straits. Other factors will, of course, continue to deter Peking, including the loss of Soviet deterrent power.

As Chinese nuclear power grows, the United States may become more cautious. On the strategic level, the President and his advisers will be confronted with the realization that in any Asian crisis they will be up against a nuclear power capable of wreaking great nuclear destruction in Asia and at least limited nuclear destruction in the United States. This fact would appear to provide some pressure against greater American involvement in Asian crises, although, of course, it is not a total determinant of what American policy would be. There has been much debate about whether a Chinese-oriented ABM system would change this situation. The Johnson and Nixon administrations argued that the credibility of American commitments in Asia would be enhanced by deploying an ABM system that could provide protection against Chinese ICBMs. Others have argued that it would be dangerous for the United States might be reluctant to concentrate its troops in a work. They also point out that Peking could still destroy American bases in East Asia and threaten to destroy America's Asian allies.

The development of the Chinese nuclear capability may impose on the United States some tactical caution as well. For example, the United States might be reluctant to concentrate its troops in a few places, as it appears now to be doing in South Vietnam, when the Chinese have a nuclear force that could destroy these concentrated installations very quickly. Although there are a number of reasons to believe that China would never use its nuclear weapons in this way, the existence of this capability would almost certainly have some effect on American deployment.

Perhaps other countries in Asia may become less confident of American willingness to accept the use of American nuclear weapons in a situation in which a nuclear war may be reciprocal.

The already limited usefulness of American nuclear power in Asia may be further eroded as China develops its own nuclear capability. This fact must be considered by the United States in assessing what is likely to be an efficacious policy in the 1970's and 1980's.

Korea

Should the United States maintain a security relationship with South Korea? If the United States had never signed a security treaty with Korea and had not fought in the Korean War, would it now want to commit itself to the defense of South Korea? This is not a real issue. President Nixon's 1970 state of the world message indicated that the United States has reviewed its commitments to South Korea and has found them consistent with American interests. Moreover, there is little public agitation in the United States or pressure from significant political groups to end the security relationship with the republic of South Korea. Barring a more fundamental change in American attitudes than now appears likely, the United States is unlikely to give any significant consideration in the next decade to the termination of the relationship. Rather, the question will be how the United States interprets and meets its obligations to South Korea, and the answer will depend upon an analysis of the threats to South Korean security.

Several threats to the security of South Korea are at least conceivable. Perhaps the least likely is the threat of nuclear attack or nuclear blackmail from China or the Soviet Union. Neither country shows any signs of engaging in nuclear blackmail, and neither appears to have interests in South Korea tthat might lead to such threats — unless, of course, the South Koreans move north and threaten the existence of the North Korean government.

The most serious threat to the security of South Korea would be an all-out surprise North Korean–Chinese invasion. Such an attack seems extremely unlikely, in part because North Korean–Chinese relations are not exceptionally close, and in any case the Chinese have not shown any proclivity for such a high-risk policy.

A North Korean invasion of South Korea cannot be ruled out, given the strong desire of the North Koreans to unify Korea under their control and the fact that the government has shown signs of recklessness and willingness to run high risks. The military balance appears to be most critical to the deterrence of such an attack.

Perhaps more likely is an inadvertent conventional war between the two countries, which results not from a deliberate decision of the North to invade the South or indeed of the South to invade the North, but rather grows out of border incidents and clashes at the demilitarized zone. Such an event is, of course, hard to deter. The outcome would depend heavily on the nature of the military balance.

The most likely threats to Korean security involve border probes, the landing of North Korean agents in South Korean territory, and an effort by the North Koreans to support active insurgency groups living in the South. The North Koreans launched a subversive campaign using these techniques in the late 1960's. By 1970 such incidents had declined, perhaps in part because the North Koreans recognized their lack of success. However, those activities could easily be resumed. The South Korean ability to handle such events depends in part on military technology, including boats fast enough to intercept North Korean boats moving to land agents on the shore. However, most fundamentally it depends on the continuing ability of the South Korean government to maintain the allegiance and loyalty of its people. So far the South Koreans have shown their determination to report all landings and foreign agents in their territory and to cooperate actively with the government in suppressing them. Continuing economic growth and a sense of political participation will probably be critical in maintaining these attitudes.

The basic policy of the Nixon administration toward Korea will presumably develop within the framework of the Nixon Doctrine. Under this policy the United States will continue to provide a nuclear umbrella over South Korea to deter threats of nuclear blackmail from the Soviet Union or China. The South Koreans will presumably be expected to carry the primary burden of conventional defense and to deal essentially on their own, with perhaps some American economic and military aid, with threats of subversion and insurgency. Given this general approach of the United States, several specific issues will arise.

An issue which has not often been discussed but which may become increasingly important is the relation of the United States nuclear posture in East Asia to the security of South Korea. The United States has agreed to respect Japanese attitudes about nuclear weapons in the postreversion period and will no longer have the right to store nuclear weapons in Okinawa. This will inevitably raise the question of the sort of nuclear posture the United States must maintain in East Asia to deter Chinese and Soviet nuclear attacks and also to contribute to the deterrence of massive conventional attack. There appears to be increasing concern in the United States over potential dangers from storing nuclear weapons overseas and thereby giving rise to the possibility of accidental or inadvertent use or the capture of the weapons by an enemy. These problems may be particularly acute in South Korea.

Because it is the policy of the United States to neither confirm nor deny the presence of nuclear weapons anywhere, except in Western Europe, there is no clear public indication of whether nuclear weapons have ever been stored in South Korea or are stored there now. Thus this issue may well be discussed, if at all, almost entirely within the United States government and secretly with the South Korean government.

The most frequently discussed and potentially critical issue in United States–South Korean security relations is whether the United States should continue to station two divisions in South Korea after the end of the Vietnam War and the return to South Korea of the Korean divisions now in South Vietnam. The Nixon Doctrine could be interpreted to mean that the United States should require the Koreans to carry the full weight of defense against a conventional North Korean attack. Moreover, as the United States defense budget declines and the number of American divisions is reduced, the need for flexibility and the ability to use forces in various places will increase pressure for the withdrawal of American forces. In July 1970 the United States informed the South Koreans that some American forces would be withdrawn from South Korea. What the United States should do must be evaluated in terms of problems of defense, deterrence, and United States–South Korean relations, in addition to the appropriate allocation of the United States defense budget and of United States ground forces.

In terms of defense against a conventional attack, a strong case can be made for the removal of all United States ground forces from South Korea. This can be done on several levels. No matter how many divisions are required for defense against North Korea, or even against a combined North Korean and Chinese attack, it is substantially cheaper to provide them from South Korean forces than from American forces. Apparently South Korean divisions fight almost as effectively as United States divisions and cost about one-tenth as much. Moreover, South Korea has sufficient manpower to field a force large enough for this purpose. In fact, it appears that the South Korean Army, augmented by their two divisions now in South Vietnam would be large enough, if assisted by United States conventional airpower and seapower, to effectively withstand a North Korean all-out attack and probably to deal with at least the initial stages of combined Chinese–North Korean attack. The South Koreans probably require additional equipment, but it is substantially cheaper to provide this than to maintain two United States divisions in South Korea.

The removal of United States divisions undoubtedly would

somewhat reduce the effectiveness of the deterrent against a North Korean attack, particularly if all the forces were withdrawn or if the United States forces that remain were withdrawn from the front line. At the present time the North Koreans know that to start a war means to shoot at Americans and that it is extremely unlikely that the United States would remain out of the conflict. But if all the United States forces were withdrawn or if those that remain withdrew from the front line, North Koreans might calculate that they could begin a war without involving the United States. Soviet ability to restrain the North Koreans might decline. At the same time, the withdrawal of all United States forces would mean the end of the United Nations command structure in Korea and would at least open the possibility that the South Koreans would be tempted to move north, particularly if their capability was increased to compensate for the American withdrawal.

The presence of American ground combat forces in South Korea also needs to be evaluated in relation to the storage of nuclear weapons in South Korea. If the United States concludes that nuclear weapons must be stored there, then it will almost certainly want ground combat troops to guard the weapons and to take care of them prior to any decision to use them.

Even if the United States decided to withdraw all its ground combat forces from South Korea, it would almost certainly want to keep some tactical airpower based there or earmarked to be moved there quickly in the event of a conflict. In view of the great expense of modern jet aircraft and the large size of the North Korean Air Force, it would be expensive to develop a South Korean Air Force able to match the capability of that of the North Koreans. Thus, an appropriate division of labor would appear to call for the South Koreans to accept most of the burden of conventional ground defense, with the United States contributing to tactical air support and providing a nuclear deterrent.

Southeast Asia after Vietnam

The Nixon Doctrine spelled out certain principles regarding the appropriate American role in Southeast Asia. The American move into Cambodia in the spring of 1970 made it clear that the full application of this doctrine would have to await the withdrawal of United States forces from South Vietnam. The Nixon Doctrine has several implications for Southeast Asia after the Vietnam War has ended.

It is easiest to begin by suggesting some of the things the United States should *not* be concerned about, or rather events for which American concern should not be translated into government action of any kind.

Violence is frequently a part of the process of political and economic change in developing countries in Asia as well as elsewhere. In some cases the violence is initiated by groups who would more effectively implement programs to develop their societies. In other cases, the violence is instigated by groups, whether on the right or left or in the center, who are corrupt and ineffective. The United States does not have the power, the wealth, or the interest to intervene whenever violence flares up within a country. The United States has no commitments to any government to keep it in power against domestic enemies not supported by external force.

The same holds true for local conflicts across borders involving states to which the United States has no security commitments. As much as the United States may deplore such activity, it cannot step in unilaterally to resolve such disputes.

Such internal conflicts and local conflicts cover much of the violence that is likely to occur in Asia and elsewhere in the developing world over the next decade, but there are residual categories left in which American action of some kind may well be needed.

The clearest need for a United States role in Southeast Asia is in relation to China's nuclear capability. In the case of overt conventional attack against countries to which the United States is committed by treaty, American interests require that the United States act. The United States cannot lightly ignore the commitments it has made. Thus, the United States does better to make its intentions clear in advance in the hopes that it can thereby deter overt aggression. But such deterrence requires that the United States maintain appropriate military forces and develop plans to use them.

American treaty commitments and concern for nonproliferation require the United States to maintain a credible deterrent against nuclear threats and conventional aggression against countries to which it is allied. In some cases the United States will wish to intervene to assist in resistance to externally supported insurgency. But a willingness on the part of the United States to intervene does not mean that it will do so automatically or without regard to what is happening in the area.

The United States attitude toward intervention as expressed in the Nixon Doctrine might well be expressed in terms of three principles: self-help, regional responsibility, and residual United States responsibility. It will be useful to examine each of these principles.

The principle of *self-help* is simply the notion that the country being threatened must take primary responsibility for its own security. In the case of conventional threats, the United States expects the country under attack to man the first line of defense. Depending on their own capability and that of potential enemies, the United States would expect them to be responsible for at least the early stages of any conflict and in some cases for the entire burden of providing ground forces. The United States would expect them, also, to maintain the necessary bases and facilities so that United States forces can return quickly when necessary, but need not remain permanently in large numbers at overseas bases.

In the case of insurgency, the United States will expect the local government to play an even more prominent role. The United States expects the local government to carry the full load of combat military operations. The United States expects them also to take primary responsibility for developing the necessary plans and programs to deal with the insurgency.

Finally, and most important, the United States expects the local government to play the primary role in those programs of political and economic development that will enable the government to build sufficient support and cohesion to effectively prevent the emergence of an insurgent group that can be effectively supported from the outside. The United States must take this attitude not only because it cannot rightly ask Americans to sacrifice if the people under direct attack are not doing their share, but also because American efforts cannot succeed unless the local forces are assuming the primary burden. Insurgency cannot be checked by an American effort.

The principle of *regional responsibility* means that the United States expects neighbors to work together to deal with the economic and political causes of instability. There have been very encouraging steps in this direction over the past several years, notably the growing number of associations for political and economic operations in Asia. To the degree that these associations are effective, the countries concerned will be in a better position to prevent the emergence of insurgency and to develop both economically and politically.

Where events reach the stage of overt insurgency, the United States hopes that the governments of the area will cooperate in providing technical assistance and advice and, where the insurgencies are located along a common border, will work together to deal with the threat. Where outside military forces are needed, the United States expects that they will be provided, at least in part, by the neighbors of the country under attack.

The third principle is that of residual United States responsibility. The United States cannot and will not do things that the nations of the region can and must do for themselves. The United States intends to keep its presence in the area at the minimum essential level. The United States itself will intervene only if its intervention is necessary and useful and important to American interests. Defining these circumstances will be the greatest challenge to American policy in Southeast Asia in the coming decades, particularly in relation to Thailand.

CHAPTER ELEVEN

ARMS CONTROL: SALT AND NPT

The search for a way to beat swords into plowshares is as old as recorded history. Ever since man first went to war, he has sought to find ways of preventing war, including the search for disarmament. Until 1960 the search for disarmament had been carried out separately from the search for security through armaments. Those who worked for disarmament did not study questions of military strategy and tended to assume that the problem was simply to get rid of weapons. On the other hand, those who were responsible for seeking security through armaments tended to view disarmament as a threat to their interests and to oppose disarmament measures. Thus, disarmament discussions were largely a utopian search for a world without weapons and were carried on largely for political propaganda purposes.

Beginning in the mid-1950's an intellectual effort was made to link efforts for disarmament with efforts to attain security by unilateral means. This activity increasingly came to be called "arms control." Those who took this approach started from the assumption that efforts to control armaments by international means and the unilateral deployment of military force had as their goal the prevention of war and the reduction of damage if war occurred, all at the lowest possible cost to society. Proponents of arms control have argued that some of the advantages that might be gained by formal international agreements could also be obtained by sensible unilateral restraint. They also argued that proposals for international agreement had to be evaluated carefully from the point of view of security to determine whether in fact they reduced the danger of war. A number of individuals who had pioneered these approaches came into the American government in 1960, and with the founding by the Kennedy administration of the Arms Control and Disarmament Agency, they gradually developed a much closer connection in the United States between arms-control efforts and unilateral military policy. In the last several years such connections appear to be developing also in the Soviet Union.

During the 1960's a number of arms-control agreements that mainly affected the United States and the Soviet Union were concluded, including the Limited Test Ban Treaty, which outlawed the testing of nuclear weapons in the atmosphere, under the sea, and in outer space; the Outer Space Treaty, which prohibited the stationing of nuclear weapons in outer space; an Antarctica Treaty, which demilitarized Antarctica and permitted inspection; and the hot-line agreement, which established a sure means of communication between Washington and Moscow for use in a major crisis. In 1968 the United States, the Soviet Union, and a number of other nations signed the nuclear Nonproliferation Treaty (NPT), designed to prevent the spread of nuclear weapons beyond the five current nuclear powers. The two nations also announced their agreement in principle to begin negotiations on strategic arms. These talks got under way in 1969.

In addition to nonproliferation and efforts to control strategic arms a number of other arms-control issues continued to be discussed. At the end of 1970 the United States and the Soviet Union had reached agreement on a treaty prohibiting the stationing of nuclear weapons on the seabed and the treaty was ready for signing. At the same time the United States and Great Britain had proposed a treaty to prohibit all biological weapons, while the Soviet Union insisted that a ban on chemical weapons had to be approved at the same time. Other methods, such as a cutoff in the production of fissionable material and an underground test ban treaty also continued to be discussed. However, the main focus is on the bilateral Strategic Arms Limitation Talks and the efforts to secure wide ratification and effectiveness for the nonproliferation treaty.

Strategic Arms Limitation Talks (SALT)

In 1968 the United States proposed to the Soviet Union that the two governments engage in secret, private negotiations to bring about a freezing of the nuclear arms race. The proposal suggested talks different from those that had been held in the past, which had been largely public and designed largely for propaganda. The Soviet government treated the proposal seriously but delayed for more than a year before agreeing to hold the talks. There followed a period of private discussion that laid the groundwork for the opening of the Strategic Arms Limitation Talks in the fall of 1968. However, in August 1968, when the Soviet Union invaded Czechoslovakia, the Johnson administration felt obliged to postpone the talks and to pass the problem on to the Nixon administration. In January 1969 the Soviet Union confirmed its willingness to proceed with the arms-limitation talks and the Nixon administration agreed in principle but indicated that it intended to develop its own position and wished to be sure that the political climate would be an appropriate one in which the talks could proceed. Preliminary talks got under way at Helsinki in the winter of 1969 and were followed by talks in Vienna in the spring of 1970. The talks proceeded in secrecy and without the propaganda that had accompanied arms-control talks in the past. Press reports indicated that both governments were engaged in serious technical discussions of leveling off the arms race.

In this section we shall review the criteria by which the two countries are likely to evaluate arms-control agreement, consider the main potential benefits of such an agreement, and review the specific kinds of agreements that may develop.

An agreement limiting the strategic offensive and defensive systems of the United States and the Soviet Union would go to the heart of the security interests of the two countries. Thus, any such agreement will be carefully evaluated by those in the military establishment and by others involved with security and the design of weapons systems, as well as by those in the Foreign Office normally involved with disarmament matters. In the most general way, both the United States and the Soviet Union would have to be convinced that an agreement protected their security and that it did not provide for any gross inequality in favor of the opposing side. More specifically, each side would insist that the agreement provided it with a confident deterrent capability. This means that the first three criteria of sufficiency as set forth by the Nixon administration must be met, viz. assured destruction, crisis stability, and relative advantage. In this situation there is strong incentive to strike first. The amount of damage each side suffers must be essentially the same no matter which side strikes first. If there is a strong incentive to strike first, then one or both sides may be tempted to consider a first strike out of fear that the other side may be planning a first strike in order to reduce the damage to itself.

The calculations testing whether the agreement is satisfactory from the point of view of the security of the two sides will be made first with the assumption that the agreement will be observed fully by both sides in the manner anticipated. However, both sides will also consider the possibility of three different kinds of behavior: evasion, avoidance, and breakdown.

Avoidance relates to the fact that no arms-control agreement, no matter how comprehensive, will cover all aspects of strategic armament. Both sides will be free to pursue improvements and changes in the areas not covered by the agreement. Thus one needs to worry about ways in which one side or the other could improve its strategic capability within the legal limits of the agreement. Each side needs to ask itself whether the likely actions of the other side in the areas not covered by the agreement will produce a situation of greater or lesser strategic stability than that which would occur without an agreement. For example, if the agreement covered strategic missiles but not bombers or air defense, each side would have to examine the likely efforts of the other in producing air defense and bombers and ask itself whether it prefers that situation to one that would occur without an agreement. Concern about breakdown reflects the fact that at some point the agreement may come to an end suddenly or slowly. One side or the other may renounce the agreement, or extraneous events such as development of a substantial nuclear capability by a third country might require the two sides to agree to end the agreement. Thus each side must ask itself what the consequences would be if the agreement breaks down. Will the other side have gotten an advantage by research and development programs or in other ways that would mean that if the agreement broke down at a particular time it might be able to develop an effective first-strike capability?

Finally, each side must worry about the problem of evasion — that is, whether the other side will violate the terms of the agreement sufficiently to upset the strategic balance. Prior to the opening of the Strategic Arms Limitation Talks the United States had always insisted that any substantial arms-control agreement had to include provisions for on-site inspection whereby Americans could visit designated sites in the Soviet Union to ensure that the agreement would be observed. However, over the last ten years the ability of the United States to verify Soviet strategic developments by unilateral means has substantially increased to the point where American officials are able to report with high confidence the number of operational Soviet missiles at any given time. For this reason American officials have indicated that it might be possible to have an arms-control agreement that required no on-sight inspection. The United States and the Soviet Union would simply by their own national means keep track of each other's compliance with an agreement. The criterion used in determining whether an agreement could be adequately verified is not whether all possibilities of cheating would be detected with 100 per cent certainty but whether there is a high probability of detecting an amount of cheating sufficient to upset the strategic balance. Both sides recognize that in the absence of an arms-control agreement the other side may be able to do things that are dangerous to the strategic balance, and therefore one has to weigh the uncertainties of some evasion of an arms-control agreement with the uncertainties of a world without an agreement.

The criteria suggested so far are the same that the United States, and presumably the Soviet Union, would use in evaluating their strategic forces in the absence of an agreement. Although both sides believe that they can maintain an effective deterrent in the absence of an agreement, they nevertheless have both indicated great interest in seeking to do so with an agreement. This is because some additional benefits could accrue from a formal agreement or a tacit understanding limiting their strategic forces.

The political implications of a formal strategic arms-control agreement between the United States and the Soviet Union have undoubtedly been important to some advocates of an agreement. Such an agreement could substantially improve the political climate between the United States and the Soviet Union and pave the way for other agreements on matters relating to security, including the security of Western Europe. Others fear that a strategic arms-control agreement would be exploited by the Soviet Union to increase the sense of concern in Western Europe about whether the United States strategic deterrent is effective against Soviets threats to Western Europe. Some suspect that this is an important Soviet motivation for seeking an agreement and that NATO might not survive a SALT agreement.

Those who favor an agreement point to the fact that in the absence of an agreement each side will feel obliged to continue to increase the size of its strategic forces. In order to defend such increases domestically, the government will be forced to justify its efforts by rhetoric implying the possibility of serious conflict between the two countries. It is argued that improved political relations are difficult in a climate in which military leaders are making strong statements about the strategic threat from the other.

Another strong motive for a formal strategic arms-limitation agreement is the likely effect on the proliferation of nuclear programs. During the course of negotiation of the Nonproliferation Treaty non-nuclear powers insisted that an operative clause be written into the treaty requiring the nuclear powers to engage in serious negotiations aimed at limiting the nuclear arms race. Many believe that the Nonproliferation Treaty will not be effective unless there is also nuclear arms limitation by the major powers. Thus, a formal agreement is seen as an important step in preventing the spread of nuclear weapons.

The desire to reduce expenditures has probably played some role in motivating interest in strategic arms limitation. This appears to be particularly the case in the Soviet Union. Soviet political leaders must be concerned about the growing pressure on the strategic arms budget coming from the growing sluggishness of the Soviet economy and the growing demand for consumer goods, as well as the need for increased expenditures for General Purpose Forces, in light of the Soviet invasion of Czechoslovakia and the growing military tensions on the Sino-Soviet border. Strategic arms expenditures are a significant part of the Soviet defense budget and use a substantial portion of the available resources of advanced technology, including computers. Soviet leaders have suggested that the desire to save money is an important component of their interest in strategic arms limitation. Cost appears to be much less important in the United States. The strategic forces cost approximately $15 billion per year and are therefore less than one-third of the defense budget. Moreover, it is unlikely that a strategic arms-limitation agreement would permit a reduction of more than $3 billion or $4 billion in strategic spending. Such an amount could more easily be saved from the much larger General Purpose Forces budget. Nevertheless, in the absence of an arms-control agreement it is possible that strategic expenditures in the United States would greatly increase over the next ten years, and this increase would be difficult to finance in view of the increasing pressure on the defense budget.

Another motive for seeking to regulate the arms race by formal international agreement is to reduce the great uncertainties in the arms competition. Both the United States and the Soviet Union know reasonably well what strategic forces the other side has at any given time, and the Soviet Union has a considerable amount of information about the future strategic intentions of the United States. However, in the absence of an agreement the Soviet leaders could not be sure whether the United States will build a new manned bomber or a large ABM system over the next six or seven years. The United States knows even less about the future strategic plans of the Soviet Union. Thus, each side must find ways to hedge against the possibility that the other side will engage in a rapid buildup of its strategic forces in the future. This uncertainty forces each side to build more than it would build if it had good knowledge of the other side's intentions and in turn stimulates greater expenditures by the other side. A formal agreement that would give each side higher confidence in the other's intentions could reduce these uncertainties, which lead to unnecessary expenditures and generate fear of what the other side may be doing.

Perhaps the most important argument for formal arms-control agreement is that it would reduce the probability of nuclear war. This is so if an agreement can prevent developments that would make war more likely. From this perspective, interest focuses primarily on two new developments in the strategic arms race — MIRVs and ABMs. Most analysts have argued that a strategic arms-control agreement should be designed to prevent deployment of MIRVs and ABMs because introduction of either would make nuclear war more likely. ABMs increase the probability of war by giving one side or the other the illusion that it could survive a retaliatory strike. MIRVs affect stability by creating an incentive to strike first. Either side with a MIRV force might be able to destroy the fixed land-based missiles of the other side. There is no question that both MIRVs and ABMs, and particularly the two of them in combination, would increase the probability of war according to strategic calculations, and hence an agreement that prohibited one or both systems could serve to reduce the probability of war.

However, neither American nor Soviet political leaders are likely to make a decision to go to nuclear war on the basis of strategic calculations. The top political leaders of both sides understand that both nations would be destroyed in a nuclear war. Neither side would start a war on the belief that it could suffer relatively less damage than the other side. Only if the political leaders came to believe that there was a substantial chance of escaping without any damage, and if they believed that the alternative to beginning a nuclear war was horrendous, would they consider the possibility of launching a preemptive first strike.

From this perspective, the key to avoiding nuclear war is to avoid a situation in which a harassed and panicky political leader might, during a severe crisis, allow himself to be convinced by his advisers that he could start a nuclear war and suffer no damage. An arms-control agreement should be designed to prevent this situation from occurring. At the present time it is clear that no political leader could possibly be convinced that after a first strike he would not suffer heavy damage in return. If one looks at possible future changes in technology, it is clear that only with a large ABM system might a political leader be persuaded that he could escape damage. Having spent large sums on a ballistic-missile defense system and having been told by those advocating such expenditures that the system would work effectively, political leaders easily come to overestimate the efficacy of ballistic-missile defense. In a time of crisis they might be told that the first strike would penetrate the enemy's ABM system because it would be large enough to saturate the defense. The enemy's counterstrike, however, would be sufficiently small that the ABM system would provide an impenetrable shield, shooting down all the incoming missiles. Although such an evaluation would almost certainly overestimate the technical capabilities of an ABM system, political leaders, led over time to believe that ABMs worked effectively, might be persuaded of this belief. MIRVs by themselves pose no such danger, for no political leader would believe that a first strike would destroy all the enemy's strategic offensive capability; certainly it could not destroy his sea-based missiles. From this perspective, the most important purpose of a strategic arms-limitation agreement would be to ban the development of ballistic missiles on both sides.

Types of Agreement

In preparation for the Strategic Arms Limitation Talks with the Soviet Union the American government reported that it considered a wide range of possible agreements. While the details of these preparations have not been made public, the general outlines were stated in President Nixon's state of the world message in January 1970, and the broad alternatives are clear from information in the public domain. At the Vienna sessions of the talks the United States put before the Soviets the general outlines of one possible agreement.

The broadest kind of agreement, one called for by the Senate in a resolution of the spring of 1967, would provide for a total freeze on the deployment of all strategic offensive and defensive systems. Under such an agreement neither side could deploy additional land-based missiles or additional submarines with ballistic missiles. Both sides would also have to cease the testing of multiple warheads because that is the only effective way to prevent their installation on strategic missiles. Limitations on bombers and air defense might be included under such an agreement. The basic argument in favor of this approach is that it would freeze an existing situation that both sides know to be stable and that stopping everything reduces the uncertainties inherent in a partial freeze. Opponents argue that it is not possible to impose effective limits on MIRVs because the testing of MIRVs cannot be monitored by unilateral means. Thus any such agreement would require on-site inspection, which is almost certainly unacceptable to the Soviet Union.

A second form of agreement would focus on freezing offensive strategic missiles at current levels and banning or severely limiting ABMs while not imposing any limits on MIRVs or other improvements in technology. This form of agreement would accept the fact that MIRV limitations are unlikely, either because the United

States has already begun deployment of MIRVs or because a MIRV ban cannot be verified. If any ABMs are to be permitted on each side, under such an agreement it would have to be limited to specific areas, such as the capitals of the two countries. This is because if both sides were to deploy radars covering their entire country, they could quickly convert a small ABM system into a large ABM system. Given that the Soviet Union has an ABM system deployed about Moscow and given the American interest in some sort of ABM deployment, it is possible that an agreement would focus on freezing the number of strategic offensive launchers and limiting ABMs to defense of the two national capitals. A variation of such an agreement would permit the United States and the Soviet Union to substitute sea-based for land-based forces by freezing only the total number of strategic offensive missiles. This was the form of agreement.

A third form of agreement would permit MIRVs and area ABM systems but would seek to limit the number of ABMs while freezing the number of fixed land-based and sea-based offensive missiles. Although such an agreement would not prohibit the introduction of either MIRVs or ABMs, it would put a limit on the arms race, preventing large ABM systems from being deployed and preventing the introduction of new strategic offensive systems.

A final form of agreement would focus simply on one strategic system at a time — for example, freezing fixed land-based missiles or the number of sea-based missiles.

Whether it will in fact be possible to negotiate any agreement remains to be seen. Even if the two sides could agree in principle on the desirability of a particular agreement, there would remain long and difficult negotiating of the precise terms. Thus it is possible that any agreement would first be negotiated in an informal way. Each side would inform the other of an intention — for example, to freeze the number of offensive missiles and not build ABM systems beyond those protecting the capital. Each side could then observe for itself if the other was living up to what it said it would do. Over time the informal agreement could be turned into a formal treaty.

The danger remains that Strategic Arms Limitation Talks will lead to no agreement and will provide a rationale and cover for increases in the strategic forces of both sides. For example, the United States has justified proceeding with the ABM system as necessary to give it a bargaining chip for the negotiations.

Nonproliferation of Nuclear Weapons

The treaty to prevent the proliferation of nuclear weapons went into effect in 1970 when the United States, the Soviet Union, and forty other nations ratified it. The treaty obligates the nuclear powers — the United States, the Soviet Union, Great Britain, France, and China — not to transfer nuclear weapons to any non-nuclear power or to otherwise assist in developing nuclear weapons. It also obligates the non-nuclear nations not to produce nuclear weapons and to put their nuclear reactors and all fissionable material developed for peaceful purposes under the supervision of the International Atomic Energy Agency. Thus far a number of potential nuclear powers including West Germany and Japan have signed the treaty but have not ratified it, whereas others such as Australia and India have yet to sign. Whether the treaty will be effective in the long run depends on whether most of the potential nuclear powers sign it and also on whether successful negotiations can be carried on between these countries and the IAEA to bring the verification procedures into effect.

Some analysts argue that it would be good for other countries such as Japan to develop their own nuclear capability as a balance against China, and others have argued that the European nations as a group should have nuclear weapons. However, most analysts and the governments of the major powers have accepted that the further spread of nuclear weapons will contribute to international instability. The more nations that have nuclear weapons the more likely it is that somehow they will be used in a military conflict. It is also the case that arms control will be much more difficult if there are many nuclear powers.

From the point of view of potential nuclear nations, however, the problem is different. For each country the question is not whether the general spread of nuclear weapons is desirable, but whether a nuclear capability is necessary for its security or sense of national pride. India, which feels threatened by China and in which there is a growing sense of nationalism, is almost certain not to sign the Nonproliferation Treaty, although it may not develop a nuclear capability. The Israelis are unlikely to sign the treaty unless there is a political settlement in the Middle East, but they too may hold off from getting nuclear weapons. Japan, on the other hand, may ratify the treaty but may in the future feel obliged to renounce the agreement as the Chinese nuclear capability grows, if they come to feel that American nuclear protection is incompatible with their sense of nationalism. In each of these countries and in others, the strategic arguments will be used in an internal political debate in which the question of nuclear weapons will come to be a symbol of nationalism, of independence from the United States, or of an effective role in the world. The Nonproliferation Treaty by itself does not prevent nuclear spread. What the treaty does is to create a framework in which the debate within particular potential nuclear powers will be carried out. The existence of the treaty may in some cases strengthen those opposed to developing a nuclear capability. The treaty also provides a framework in which the United States and the Soviet Union — in the context of seeking support for an international treaty rather than in the context of bilateral political pressures — can urge countries not to go nuclear. The inspection procedures provided by the treaty are more symbolic than real. Under them, all nuclear material produced for peaceful reactors will be under IAEA inspection. Some analysts argue that IAEA inspection will be virtually useless in preventing the diversion of nuclear material to clandestine weapon programs and that the existence of the IAEA safeguards may lead to a false sense of security under which nuclear reactors would be widely dispersed.

Preventing the spread of nuclear weapons will be easier if there is a strategic arms-limitation agreement between the nuclear powers and also if there is a complete test ban and a cutoff in the production of fissionable material. Such agreements may be possible if a strategic arms-limitations treaty is negotiated between the two superpowers.

SELECTED BIBLIOGRAPHY

THE ROLE OF FORCE IN THE NUCLEAR AGE

Herz, John H. *International Politics in the Atomic Age*. New York: Columbia University Press, 1959.

Kissinger, Henry A. *Nuclear Weapons and Foreign Policy*. New York: Harper and Row, 1957.

Knorr, Klaus. *On the Uses of Military Power in the Nuclear Age*. Princeton, N.J.: Princeton University Press, 1966.

Osgood, Robert E. and Tucker, Robert W. *Force, Order and Justice*. Baltimore: Johns Hopkins Press, 1967.

Schelling, Thomas C. *Arms and Influence*. New Haven: Yale University Press, 1966.

Tucker, Robert W. *The Just War*. Baltimore: Johns Hopkins Press, 1960.

Waltz, Kenneth N. *Man, the State, and War*. New York: Columbia University Press, 1959.

WARFARE IN THE NUCLEAR AGE

Aron, Raymond. *The Great Debate*. Garden City, N.Y.: Doubleday, 1965.

Brown, Neville. *Nuclear War: The Impending Strategic Deadlock.* London: Pall Mall Press, 1964.

McNamara, Robert S. *The Essence of Security: Reflections in Office.* New York: Harper and Row, 1968.

The Military Balance. Annual publication of the Institute for Strategic Studies, London.

Quester, George. *Deterrence Before Hiroshima.* New York: Wiley, 1966.

Schelling, Thomas C. *The Strategy of Conflict.* Cambridge, Mass.: Harvard University Press, 1960.

Statement by Secretary of Defense to House and Senate Armed Services Committees (annually); available in the Budget Hearings of the House and Senate Armed Services Committees and since 1970 from the United States Government Printing Office.

Strategic Survey. Annual publication of the Institute for Strategic Studies, London.

QUANTITATIVE AND QUALITATIVE RESEARCH METHODS

Hitch, Charles J. and McKean, Roland N. *The Economics of Defense in the Nuclear Age.* Cambridge, Mass.: Harvard University Press, 1963.

Kent, Glenn A. *On the Interaction of Opposing Forces Under Possible Arms Agreements.* Harvard Center for International Affairs, Occasional Paper No. 5. March 1963.

Planning-Programming-Budgeting; Defense Analysis: Two Examples. National Security and International Operations Subcommittee. U.S. Senate Committee on Government Operations. Washington, D.C., 1969.

Quade, Edward S., ed. *Analysis for Military Decisions.* Chicago: Rand McNally, 1964.

Wohlstetter, Albert, *et al. Selection and Use of Strategic Air Bases.* RAND Report, R-266. April 1964.

THE EVOLUTION OF AMERICAN MILITARY STRATEGY

Hammond, Paul Y. *Organizing for Defense.* Princeton, N.J.: Princeton University Press, 1961.

Huntington, Samuel P. *The Common Defense*. New York: Columbia University Press, 1961.

Kaufmann, William. *The McNamara Strategy*. New York: Harper and Row, 1964.

Schilling, Warner R., Hammond, Paul Y., and Snyder, Glenn H. *Strategy, Politics, and Defense Budgets*. New York: Columbia University Press, 1962.

SOVIET MILITARY STRATEGY

Dinerstein, Herbert S., Gouré, Leon, and Wolfe, Thomas W., eds. *Soviet Military Strategy*. Englewood Cliffs, N.J.: Prentice-Hall, 1963.

Dinerstein, Herbert S. *War and the Soviet Union*. New York: Praeger, 1959.

Garthoff, Raymond L. *Soviet Military Policy*. New York: Praeger, 1966.

Horelick, Arnold, and Rush, Myron. *Strategic Power and Soviet Foreign Policy*. Chicago: University of Chicago Press, 1966.

Mackintosh, Malcolm. *Strategy and Tactics of Soviet Foreign Policy*. London: Oxford University Press, 1962.

Wolfe, Thomas W. *Soviet Strategy at the Crossroads*. Cambridge, Mass.: Harvard University Press, 1964.

CHINESE MILITARY STRATEGY

Halperin, Morton H. *China and the Bomb*. New York: Praeger, 1965.

Halperin, Morton H., and Perkins, Dwight H. *Communist China and Arms Control*. New York: Praeger, 1965.

Hinton, Harold. *Communist China in World Politics*. Boston: Houghton Mifflin, 1966.

Hsieh, Alice. *Communist China's Strategy in the Nuclear Age*. Englewood Cliffs, N.J.: Prentice-Hall, 1962.

Huck, Arthur. *The Security of China: Chinese Approaches to War and Strategy*. New York: Columbia University Press, 1969.

Tsou, Tang, ed. *China in Crisis: China's Policies in Asia and American Alternatives*. Chicago: University of Chicago Press, 1968.

Whiting, Allen. *China Crosses the Yalu*. New York: Macmillan, 1960.

GENERAL WAR: THE STRATEGY OF SUFFICIENCY

Brodie, Bernard. *Strategy in the Missile Age*. Princeton, N.J.: Princeton University Press, 1959.

Rathjens, George W. *The Future of the Strategic Arms Race*. New York: Carnegie Endowment for International Peace, 1969.

Snyder, Glenn H. *Deterrence and Defense*. Princeton, N.J.: Princeton University Press, 1961.

LIMITED WAR: THE NATURE OF THE LIMITING PROCESS

Halperin, Morton H. *Limited War in the Nuclear Age*. New York: Wiley, 1963.

Kissinger, Henry A. *Nuclear Weapons and Foreign Policy*. New York: Harper and Row, 1957.

Osgood, Robert E. *Limited War: The Challenge to American Strategy*. Chicago: University of Chicago Press, 1957.

DETERRENCE AND DEFENSE IN EUROPE

Buchan, Alastair, and Windsor, Philip. *Arms and Stability in Europe*. London: Chatto and Windus, 1963.

Enthoven, Alain C., and Smith, Wayne K. "What Forces for NATO and From Whom?" *Foreign Affairs*. October 1969, pp. 80–96.

Kissinger, Henry A. *The Troubled Partnership*. New York: McGraw-Hill, 1965.

Osgood, Robert E. *NATO: The Entangling Alliance*. Chicago: University of Chicago Press, 1962.

Richardson, James L. *Germany and the Atlantic Alliance*. Cambridge, Mass.: Harvard University Press, 1966.

Stanley, Timothy. *NATO in Transition*. New York: Praeger, 1965.

DETERRENCE AND DEFENSE IN ASIA

Barnett, A. Doak. *Communist China and Asia*. New York: Harper and Row, 1960.

Buchan, Alastair, ed. *China and the Peace of Asia*. New York: Praeger, 1965.

Greene, Fred. *United States Policy and the Security of Asia*. New York: McGraw-Hill, 1960.

Jordon, Amos. *Foreign Aid and the Security of Southeast Asia*. New York: Praeger, 1962.

Kennedy, D. E. *The Security of Southern Asia*. London: Chatto and Windus, 1965.

ARMS CONTROL: SALT AND NPT

Bull, Hedley. *The Control of the Arms Race.* New York: Praeger, 1965.

Levine, Robert A. *The Arms Debate.* Cambridge, Mass.: Harvard University Press, 1963.

Schelling, Thomas C., and Halperin, Morton H. *Strategy and Arms Control.* New York: The Twentieth Century Fund, 1961.

Scoville, Herbert, Jr. *Toward a Strategic Arms Limitation Agreement.* New York: Carnegie Endowment for International Peace, 1970.

Stone, Jeremy J. *Containing the Arms Race.* Cambridge, Mass.: M.I.T. Press, 1966.

INDEX

ABM (Anti-Ballistic Missile), 3, 4, 16, 21, 50, 51, 53, 59, 63, 73, 79–81, 83–85, 86, 119, 135, 136, 137–139
Acheson, Dean, 40, 43
aircraft carriers, 26
Albania, 65
Antarctica Treaty, 129
Arab-Israeli War, 7
arms control, 128–140
Arms Control and Disarmament Agency, 45, 129
assured deterrence, 21, 49, 52–53, 72, 73–76
Australia, 139
Austria, 101
Aviation Week, 55

B52 bomber, 4
Bay of Pigs, 19
Berlin, 15, 100
bombers, 33
Bowles, Chester, 43
Budget Bureau, 51

Cambodia, 17
CEP (Circular Error Probability), 2–3
China, 17, 59, 69, 72, 79–81, 84, 88, 90, 93, 113–120, 121
CIA (Central Intelligence Agency), 51
Clifford, Clark, 30
contingencies, 26, 51–52
crises, 6–7, 15, 72, 76–77
Cuban missile crisis, 7, 14, 15, 17, 18, 36–37, 89, 95
cultural revolution, 63
Czechoslovakia, 18, 100, 101, 130

Defense Program Review Committee, 51
détente, 6, 99–100
domino theory, 89

Dulles, John Foster, 25, 43, 44

Eisenhower, Dwight, 41, 45
escalation, 19

Finland,101
flexible response, 109–111
Foreign Affairs, 46
Foster, William C., 45

Gaither Committee, 45–47
Germany, 105, 139
Greece, 100
Green Berets, 50

Haiphong, 17
Hamburg, 100, 101
Hanoi, 114
Hiroshima, 2
hot line, 24
Hungary, 7, 18, 101

IAEA (International Atomic Energy Agency), 139, 140
inadvertent nuclear war, 12–13
India, 96, 116, 118, 139
Israel, 140
ISS (Institute for Strategic Studies), 55

Japan, 70, 115, 117, 130, 139, 189
Johnson, Lyndon, 48, 58, 73, 94
Joint Chiefs of Staff, 84–85

Kaufman, William, 43
Kennedy, John, 45, 47, 50, 129
Khrushchev, Nikita, 6, 58
kiloton, 2
Kissinger, Henry, 43
Kong Le, 18
Korea, 7, 18, 27, 40–41, 42, 70, 89, 90, 93, 94, 95, 96, 97, 99, 115, 118, 120–124

Laird, Melvin, 30, 84
Laos, 18
limited war, 10–11, 16–19

McNamara, Robert, 30, 47, 49, 73, 83
Mao Tse-tung, 63, 70
massive retaliation, 25, 43–45, 102–103
megaton, 2
Military Strategy, 54–55
minimum deterrence, 20–21
Minuteman, 4, 16, 30, 49, 84, 85–86
MIRV (Multiple Independently Targeted Re-entry Vehicle), 3, 4, 16, 50, 58, 59, 75, 77, 83, 135, 136, 137–138
"missile gap," 47

National Security Council, 40, 51
NATO (North Atlantic Treaty Organization), 27, 35–36, 39, 41, 42, 48–49, 56, 59–61, 99–112, 133
Nitze, Paul, 40
Nixon, Richard, 26, 30, 47, 73, 83, 137, 194
Nixon Doctrine, 51, 122, 124–127
Norstad, Lauris, 107
Norway, 100
NPT (Nonproliferation Treaty), 139–140
NSC–68, 39–40, 45
Nuclear Planning Group, 105

Okinawa, 122

Outer Space Treaty, 129

Pakistan, 96
"paper tiger," 66
PLA (People's Liberation Army), 63
Polaris, 49
Poseidon, 4

Quemoy, 64, 97, 118

Radford, Arthur, 41
RAND Corporation, 28, 34, 46, 55
Rockefeller Brothers Fund, 46

SALT (Strategic Arms Limitation Talks), 6, 53, 59, 129, 130–139, 140
Seabed Treaty, 129
"self-help," 126
Senate, 53, 137
Sino-Soviet relations, 61–62, 68–69
Sokolovsky, Soviet General, 54
Soviet Union, 2, 3, 4, 5, 15–16, 22, 30, 45, 49, 55–59, 88, 90, 93, 100–101, 134, 138
spasm war, 11–12
Sputnik, 45
Suez, 19
sufficiency, 51, 72, 131
Sweden, 101
systems analysis, 29, 48
Systems Analysis, Office of, 111

tactical nuclear weapons, 5, 42, 49, 95–96, 103–107, 108, 122
Taiwan, 18, 64, 65, 70, 116, 117, 118
Test Ban, 129, 140
Thailand, 127
Tibet, 18, 65, 116
Titan, 4, 49
Tollinn system, 56
"trip-wire" signal, 102
Truman, 38, 40, 42, 43
Turkey, 100

U–2, 61, 100
United Kingdom, 5–6, 105
United Nations General Assembly, 116

verification, 132–133
Vietnam, 17, 18, 48, 50, 89, 93, 94, 95, 96, 114

Wiesner, Jerome, 45
Wohlstetter, Albert, 46

Yugoslavia, 101